THE ROCKHOUND'S HANDBOOK

By James R. Mitchell

The Rockhound's Handbook
Copyright © 1996   Gem Guides Book Co.
                315 Cloverleaf Drive, Suite F
                Baldwin Park, CA 91706

Illustrations and Cover: Mark Webber
Published in the United States of America

Library of Congress Catalog Number: 96-77412
ISBN 0-935182-90-X

□ TABLE OF CONTENTS

□ INTRODUCTION

Interest in gems dates back to prehistory. Colorful pebbles and glistening crystals, with their often perfect geometric proportions, were gathered and kept as treasured objects. They were used for personal adornment and, eventually, the finer examples became symbols of wealth and social status.

Through the ages, colored stones and crystals were not only relished for their beauty but they also embodied religious, medical and superstitious significance. Some became agents of good fortune, while others were believed capable of warding off intruders, thereby symbolizing safety and security. They were thought to be "cures" for various diseases or even capable of predicting the future. In fact, to this day, many of these superstitions and beliefs prevail.

Fundamentally, minerals are the basic materials forming all rocks which make up the earth. Each mineral has a specific chemical and orderly internal structure, resulting from the way its particular atoms and molecules group and align themselves. That precise and symmetric inner arrangement often manifests itself in the form of solid geometric treasures, bounded by planes which intersect at specific angles, known as crystals. Some minerals, when allowed to "grow" unobstructed and without the influx of impurities, form crystals which are often remarkably symmetric. Some clusters are so precise and intricate that even the most skilled craftsman would not be able to create anything comparable. Remarkably, they are the product of natural forces, some of which were violent beyond comprehension.

Until recent times, the finest gemstones and crystals were the possessions of only the most elite and wealthy. The average person might have had a few colorful stones which they found or bartered for, but most were beyond the means of anybody but the rich. To maintain the value and rarity of the most prized minerals, their sources were seldom revealed. In fact, anyone involved with these early mining projects faced the real threat of death if even suspected of divulging the location of a prime deposit. In addition, the techniques for extracting minerals from their place in the surrounding rock without damage, or crafting the gems into jewelry, were guarded secrets held within families or small communities.

In more recent times, however, things have changed. Granted, locations where the very finest minerals and gemstones can be found are still protected by laws and even weapons, but amateurs now have a much better opportunity to gather specimens on their own. This shift results from the countless books that have become available during the past half-century. These publications cover virtually every aspect of mineral collection, from theories of formation, extraction techniques, and field-trip guides, to cutting, polishing, and preservation. There are guidebooks, filled with maps, that direct the aspiring collector to mineral-bearing locations in just about any part of the United

States or Canada, and, to a lesser degree, to just about any part of the world. Some of the best field guides provide detailed descriptions about the sites, driving instructions, site-specific collecting tips, and photographs. No longer are the sources a secret!

PHOTO 1 *Rock and mineral collecting offers many opportunities to see areas that few others ever visit, such as the Bisti Badlands in New Mexico.*

Most beginners initially develop their interest in minerals by either accompanying someone on a field trip, or using a gem trail guidebook to direct them to productive sites. That aspect of the hobby, involving the actual searching for gems and minerals, is also referred to as rockhounding. As rockhounds or gem hunters become more involved with the hobby, curiosity about how to better identify minerals and, ultimately, how to cut, polish, and make jewelry from their finds generally follows. The actual crafting of gems and minerals is more specifically known as lapidary, and that branch of the hobby encompasses all aspects of polishing stones and jewelry making.

The interest in lapidary usually results from the need to "touch up" specimens found in the field in order to best exhibit their beautiful colors or crystal structure. Crystal clusters often contain sections which are broken or badly fractured. Those regions must be trimmed away, leaving only the best of the lot. Solid material is usually dirty and dull because the surface has been abraded by the forces of nature, and should be cleaned and polished to show its true beauty. That isn't to say you will be disappointed with what can be found. It just means that no mineral will be as attractive as that which is displayed in museums or set in jewelry unless some work is done to it. What you see in mineral stores, museums, and beautifully illustrated books has been carefully cleaned, trimmed, repaired, and/or polished.

When I first got involved with mineral collecting, I followed the above scenario precisely. My first trips to the field were restricted to known and popular locations, either shown to me by experienced collectors or the result of a self-guided tour described in a magazine or book. As my interest progressed, curiosity intensified in relation to how the locations were originally discovered. Did someone just stumble upon the minerals as they were hiking through the area, or were there features of the land or other clues that lead them to those spots?

Eventually, I began to read about minerals, primarily in regard to their formation, and began to understand why certain situations and settings provided a better chance for producing quality specimens than others. That knowledge helped increase my success level when at known collecting sites and has even allowed me to actually discover deposits on my own. It is fun, when driving down a highway, or traveling along some dusty dirt road in the hinterlands, to see something in the surrounding countryside, or to spot a suspect rock formation, or a geological situation that makes me curious. Sometimes that curiosity has helped me find some excellent minerals. It is my hope that the following pages will describe to you some of those intuitive situations so you, too, will be more successful on your collecting trips.

At this point it is very important that you not be mislead into thinking that top quality minerals are easy to find. Do not set unreasonable expectations. The chance of ever coming upon a museum quality gemstone or crystal formation is slim. Usually such pieces are only found deep within mines and it takes huge investments of money for equipment, as well as skilled personnel, to get to them. Obviously, any mine currently being worked is completely off limits, since the owners have a huge investment in the project. Old and abandoned prospects might have some mineralogical potential, but are usually so unstable and dangerous that the risks are not worth the slim possibility of finding something. Even if there are reports of nice crystals or minerals deep within an old rotten mine, their value is certainly not worth risking your life.

Don't let this discourage you, though, since mines are only constructed where the minerals and gemstones are of such a high concentration and/or quality that the huge outlay of money, versus their value, makes the effort worthwhile. Lesser concentrations or a more widely scattered deposit may not be worth the expense. Those unprofitable locations are where the rockhounds, armed with their small tools and a willingness to do some work, can still find lots of nice specimens.

Beyond having a chance to gather interesting material, gem and mineral collecting offers numerous supplementary positives. It is an excellent family activity, where even youngsters have an equal chance of discovering a treasure lying on the ground or in a small crack or cavity. It also provides an excuse to get away from bustle of the city, breathe clean air, and explore scenic, pristine, and often remote areas which few others ever see.

This book attempts to serve as a springboard into rockhounding and lapidary. It is primarily addressed to the beginner, and contains enough practical information to get anyone started. Most books on the market are far too complex and technical to be of any practical use to beginners or they are so elementary that they serve no functional purpose. A novice doesn't need a mining book or a complete course in geology or mineralogy. The underlying premise of this book is an assumption that the reader does not know much about gem and mineral collecting or lapidary, but is intelligent enough to want some assistance beyond the most fundamental and sometimes obvious.

Within the following pages are tips and suggestions, accompanied by numerous photographs, which should help you with field collecting and fundamental lapidary. More advanced books related to any or all topics are available when you get to a point where you need more information. It is also suggested that you consider joining a club or taking a class to assist in your progress. Hopefully, this text will also be of use to

PHOTO 2 *Rockhounding is a hobby that can be shared by the whole family.*

advanced collectors as a reliable reference containing helpful, solid knowledge in an easy-to-locate format.

An attempt has been made to organize the book in a meaningful manner. First, there is a very basic discussion about how rocks and minerals are formed, followed by helpful suggestions in regard to preparing for your field trips. Next, is a discussion of the most commonly encountered gems and minerals with instructions for identification. Don't worry, nothing extremely technical, just fundamentals which should make your trips more productive. The text continues by providing collecting tips and suggestions for actually finding and gathering specimens, followed by a short treatise about laws governing collecting and mining claims. The second part of the book furnishes a look at how to prepare and preserve your specimens. It is followed by brief instructions related to the most basic aspects of lapidary, including tumbling, cutting and polishing, faceting, and jewelry making.

A major frustration I envision with this book is that it will eventually be "outgrown" since there isn't enough detailed information on any single topic to get beyond the essentials. But, again, the purpose is to deliver enough information to get you off to a good start and provide a taste of the hobby without overwhelming you with too many facts and details. It is for someone just wanting to "test the waters" but wanting to test those waters with some chance of success.

Each chapter provides a good overview related to the particular topic being covered. The chapter on making jewelry, for example, is in no way intended to give every detail related to jewelry making, settings, and silversmithing. Such a book could potentially be hundreds or even thousands of pages in length. The chapter on mineral identification only talks about those minerals most commonly encountered by beginning collectors and completely leaves out sophisticated gemstone identification tests which a more advanced rockhound might want to conduct.

A good selection of books and periodicals related to whichever aspect(s) of rockhounding and/or lapidary you want to pursue in greater detail are listed in Appendix E. In addition, there are many magazines (also listed in Appendix E) devoted to gem and mineral collecting, lapidary and jewelry making which not only contain helpful articles and tips, but also advertisements, book reviews, and photographs which can be of great help.

I also suggest that you actually read the glossary. That may sound very tedious, but knowing the terminology and reading the definitions will greatly enhance your knowledge. In addition, as you read the text, be sure to refer to the glossary if you come upon a term you do not understand. The book will lose its practicality if you can't comprehend what is being talked about.

Probably the greatest excitement related to rockhounding is the ever present possibility of making a new find or discovery of importance. There are few other hobbies as rewarding, even if you don't find a museum piece. Gem and mineral collecting is like going on a treasure hunt. There is the excitement of pursuit, the research and "strategy," the planning and preparation, and the unknown. Will you find something? Will it make your efforts worthwhile? Digging into a cavity or excavating a pit for a mineral specimen is just like opening a package that has been sealed for millions of years. You don't know what will be inside, but it could be something magnificent.

Once you get your "treasures" home, the excitement continues when their natural beauty is enhanced by trimming, polishing, cleaning and/or setting in jewelry. It is an intellectually stimulating hobby which can lead to additional study of mineralogy, geology, chemistry, physics, and, as a side, even paleontology and astronomy. Use this book as it is intended - as a starting point. It supplies lots of ideas and helpful tips. If you employ the suggestions included within these covers, you will be well on your way to what could be a lifetime hobby filled with excitement and satisfaction.

CHAPTER 1 ROCK & MINERAL FORMATION

Before you start planning your first collecting trip, it is important to have a basic understanding of how rocks and minerals are formed. Don't panic! A technical full-fledged course in geology and mineralogy is not necessary to assure a productive and enjoyable trip. Some of the fundamentals, however, will help to enhance your chances of finding the best a particular site has to offer. Even when in a region known for minerals, an understanding of how the surrounding terrain came into existence may help steer you to better mineral concentrations and the finest specimens. With that buildup, how can you even consider not reading the rest of this chapter? So . . . take a deep breath and read on.

Before getting too far, however, let us first examine the difference between rocks and minerals. As mentioned in the introduction, minerals are naturally occurring compounds which possess specific chemical and physical properties. Each individual mineral is also characterized by its unique orderly internal structure, resulting from the way the particular atoms and molecules group and align themselves. Gold, silver, calcite, quartz, and garnet are all examples of minerals. Rocks, on the other hand, are simply aggregates of more than one mineral, thereby exhibiting no specific, singular, chemical or atomic make-up. Granite, marble, sandstone, and obsidian are examples of rocks, each made up of many minerals.

□ ROCKS

For the most part, rocks are not as highly prized by collectors as minerals. They lack chemical purity, generally possess a non-uniform internal structure, are usually grainy, and seldom crystallize. The study of rocks, however, is important to collectors, since it is within rock that the minerals are concentrated and sometimes allowed to crystallize. It is therefore very helpful to know what types of rock and under what conditions the formation of such specimens are most favorable.

There are three major rock types, the most basic being *igneous*, which comprises everything solidified from a molten, liquid state. If the molten rock cooled slowly, deep within the crust of the earth, the resulting mass usually turned out to be grainy. If it cooled rapidly, such as when ejected from a volcano into the cool air, the results were very fine grained. Generally, the best minerals are associated with the more grainy material, since the voids between the individual particles making up the rock are sometimes large enough to allow crystal growth or better concentration. Within igneous material cooled rapidly, there is no time for selective crystallization to take place and the result is volcanic glass, better known as obsidian.

PHOTO 3 *The vehicle is at the base of a small igneous mountain range situated in western Arizona.*

Igneous rocks do not show layering, they generally don't flake, they often include small gas bubbles or holes, and they contain no fossils. Don't misunderstand the part about no layering, however. Many igneous rocks exhibit apparent banding or parallel patterns which might be confused with a true plane-by-plane layering. The bands in igneous formations, however, result from the ancient molten material's flow before it solidified.

PHOTO 4 *The truck is parked next to an igneous basalt flow near Kingston, New Mexico.*

By far, the most prolific source of gemstones and perfectly formed crystals are igneous rocks. A few of the countless minerals associated with igneous rocks are silver, copper, feldspar, topaz, tourmaline and garnet. The vehicle in Photo 3 is located at the base of a small igneous mountain, while the one in Photo 4 is parked next to a basalt flow, also igneous in origin.

The second major classification is termed *sedimentary*. Sedimentary rocks result from massive accumulations of small rock and mineral grains, as well as any other debris that may have become captured in the process. Initially, the buildup is caused by natural erosive forces such as water and rain, or by the settling of particles to the bottom of lakes or seas. As the deposit increased in thickness, great pressure and temperature was imparted upon the lower portions, thereby actually cementing it into firm and solid stone.

Parallel layers are often evident in sedimentary rock, due to the way it was formed, layer upon layer, over the course of countless years. A few minerals associated with sedimentary rock include barite, calcite, opal, sulfur, and even fossils.

PHOTO 5 *A good example of a sedimentary formation in Johnson Canyon, Utah.*

Photo 5 shows a good example of a sedimentary formation. Note the distinct layering which, even though somewhat contorted, can easily be distinguished. Photo 6 illustrates another, but somewhat unusual instance of a sedimentary formation. Observe how the bedding planes in the lower portion of the mountain are tilted, a result of earth movement, while the upper region has distinctly different bedding planes. This situation is referred to as an unconformity.

The third rock classification is *metamorphic*. Metamorphic rocks are the consequence of immense heat and pressure placed on existing igneous, sedimentary or other metamorphic rocks. When those forces are sufficiently intense, the original stone will be altered into something completely different, with the internal mineral components being significantly altered and/or chemically changed. Metamorphic rocks originate from deep within the earth, since that is the only place where such extreme forces are possible. They might show distinct internal flattening, either parallel or in wavy planes. A good example of a metamorphic rock is the gneiss shown in Photo 7.

A few minerals associated with metamorphic rocks include graphite, mica, talc, asbestos, diamond, pyrite, and lead.

PHOTO 6 *A sedimentary unconformity located near San Lorenzo Arroyo, New Mexico.*

PHOTO 7 *A chunk of metamorphic rock called gneiss, found in the eastern Great Smoky Mountains of North Carolina.*

□ COMMON MINERAL-PRODUCING SITUATIONS

We will start our study of mineral formation by looking at some of the most commonly encountered situations conducive to accumulation and/or crystallization in quantities large and pure enough to be of interest to collectors. The following paragraphs present the theory, while Chapter 6 will provide tips on how to use this information while actually in the field.

Common Igneous Conditions

One of the most typical ways minerals are concentrated is based on their differing relative melting temperatures. The process takes place as a mass of molten magma begins to cool. If the temperature change is slow, minerals are able to selectively solidify. Those with higher melting points begin to separate out of the molten mass and harden, while others with lower melting points remain liquefied much longer, not being able to separate, concentrate and crystallize until the temperature had further decreased. If the process is slow enough, the resulting internal crystal structure might be significant, but usually the rock mass is so tightly packed that it is of little practical interest to collectors. Photo 8 shows such a situation, where the granite contains lots of large but solidly embedded crystals.

PHOTO 8 *Coarse granite with large, compacted crystals found near Acton, California.*

Pegmatites

One particular geological formation, referred to as a pegmatite, frequently allows for spectacular crystal growth and mineral concentration. Pegmatites originate at a time when a molten igneous mass starts to cool and harden. During that period, cracks often form in the unstable and partially solidified rock, either as a result of the cooling process itself or due to earth movement or slippage. The molten material still trapped within that recently hardened rock is sometimes squeezed into those cracks and fissures due to immense internal pressure. The result is a pegmatite. Pegmatites provide the space and the chemical isolation necessary for the formation of more pure mineral crystals. If the open area is very large, in comparison to the amount of solidifying magma, the minerals have an opportunity to sort themselves out and concentrate, while crystals have the potential to attain substantial size, sometimes exhibiting near perfect geometric proportions.

Not all molten rock is the same, however. The texture, chemistry and density of the parent magma determines the type of gems and minerals that will ultimately be present. Different types of igneous rock will offer considerably different outcomes. In spite of this apparent lack of consistency, pegmatites are generally regarded as a reliable and notable source of beautiful crystals and mineral specimens.

Within many pegmatites are pockets and other such voids. Crystals found

13

in those regions are usually layered, with the first to crystallize being closest to the wall and those later to crystallize more toward the center. It is this last-to-solidify area, called the core, that has great mineralogical consequences, since it often contains the finest, most valuable, and rarest specimens.

A pegmatite is composed of virtually the same substances as granite, but tends to be considerably more coarse. The list of what can be found in a gem pegmatite is astounding and includes spectacular quartz crystals, tourmaline, in all colors of the rainbow, beryl, feldspar, spodumene, garnet, topaz, apatite, zircon, and mica, just to name a few. Photo 9 shows a fine example of a small, light-colored pegmatite cutting through a block of igneous rock.

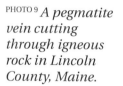

PHOTO 9 *A pegmatite vein cutting through igneous rock in Lincoln County, Maine.*

Hydrothermal Veins

Hydrothermal veins are yet another condition known for producing collectable minerals. The formation of a hydrothermal vein begins under situations similar to that of a pegmatite. The major difference being that, instead of the cracks in the surrounding rock being filled with molten magma, they were penetrated with superheated water. When that water jetted through the cracks, it carried with it dissolved minerals and metals. The temperature of the water and composition of the surrounding rock determined exactly what was involved. As the water cooled, the suspended minerals solidified, often forming beautiful crystals.

Unlike pegmatites, which are restricted to igneous conditions, hydrothermal deposits can occur in a variety of geological settings. Any place that looks like molten water could have flowed is a possible spot for some sort of hydrothermal action. That includes regions between planes in sedimentary rock or inside openings formed by the forces of folding, uplifting and buckling of the earth's crust.

Hydrothermal veins are noted for being prime sources of metal ores, including copper, silver and gold. Other minerals associated with such veins are quartz, fluorite, chalcedony, calcite, aragonite, opal, galena, pyrite, marcasite, mica, garnet, topaz, tourmaline, rhodochrosite and barite. This, of course, is only a partial listing, but it gives you an idea of the possibilities.

Photo 10 illustrates a very interesting occurrence. The white area is a portion of a gold- and quartz-bearing hydrothermal vein that ends at a fault. The continuation of the vein is located quite a distance away, farther up the line of slippage.

PHOTO 10 *The whitish area is a portion of a gold and quartz-bearing hydrothermal vein that ends in a fault. Located near the Cook Inlet of Alaska.*

Gas

Another crack-filling situation is set up when fissures, bedding planes, and cavities are permeated with super-heated gas. If that gas contains dissolved minerals, which it often does, they will deposit on the walls, often with exquisite crystallization. Sulfur is one of the best known minerals to be deposited in such a manner.

Secondary Deposits

Secondary deposits are well respected as producers of collectable minerals. They encompass any situation where mineral-bearing water has settled or was forced into already existing voids, but not as a result of immense heat and pressures that were associated with hydrothermal formations.

A classic secondary situation is set up by the hollow regions left where gas bubbles were trapped within cooling magma. In later geological times, mineral-bearing solutions seeped into those voids, completely or partially filling them. If such solutions were rich in silica, the result could be chalcedony, agate, jasper, geodes, nodules, or even opal. Similar secondary deposition is frequently encountered within gas bubbles left in volcanic ash or between the planes of sedimentary or metamorphic rocks.

A major difference between secondary deposits and hydrothermal situations is that the secondary deposits are formed well after the surrounding rock was created. The percolating mineral-rich solutions need not be super-heated and, in fact, even rain water can serve as the transport system. If the water seeps through soil or rock rich in silica, some will be dissolved and carried by the flow until it enters a void or crack where it attaches itself to the walls. Photo 11 shows seams of calcite having been secondarily deposited within limestone. The white stringers seen cutting through the cliff in Photo 12 are also secondary deposits of calcite, this time filling ancient cracks in the host igneous rock.

PHOTO 11 *Calcite secondarily deposited into seams and cracks found in limestone from Franklin County, Vermont.*

PHOTO 12 *The white stringers cutting through the cliff, south of Socorro, New Mexico, are secondary deposits of calcite filling cracks in the host igneous rock.*

16

Contact Zones

When solid rock in the earth's crust is brought almost to the melting point, it becomes unstable and many of its included minerals recrystallize into different forms. An often reliable source of this recrystallization results when already existing rock is placed in contact with molten material. The region in and around the surfaces where the magma encounters the original rock is known as a contact zone, and it is within that zone where minerals are altered and metamorphism sometimes produces spectacular results.

One excellent example of contact metamorphism is the case when molten magma comes in contact with limestone. The limestone is "cooked" and changed into marble. If there happens to be aluminum in the limestone, the intense heat may cause it to recrystallize with silica to form rubies and/or sapphires.

Two of the most common contact zone scenarios are (1) when lava flows over the existing rock (Photo 13), and (2) when extreme subsurface pressures force molten material into existing rock (Photo 14). The latter intrusion, referred to as a dike, usually enters the native rock in regions of weakness, such as pre-existing cracks or layers.

PHOTO 13 *A contact zone created by lava flowing over existing rock near El Paso, Texas.*

PHOTO 14 *A contact region in the form of a dike cutting through limestone near Rockland, Maine.*

17

In addition to the metamorphic alteration associated with a contact zone, in many instances the molten material, upon cooling, will shrink. As a consequence of this cooling it will pull slightly away from the other rock. Such spaces provide a perfect environment for subsequent hydrothermal or secondary deposition, as discussed earlier.

□ CONCLUSION

You now have a very basic understanding of the most commonly encountered rock- and mineral-producing conditions. Keep in mind, however, even when you do encounter such geological settings, that any minerals and crystals that may be present could be difficult, if not impossible, for you, the amateur collector, to obtain. It is often necessary to use heavy equipment, explosives, and other mining equipment to access the pockets, split the seams, or remove the tough surrounding rock. Occasionally, though, armed with a pry bar, rock pick, sledge hammer, and lots of energy, diligent rockhounds can expose portions of such deposits and the rewards can be substantial.

CHAPTER 2 PLANNING A FIELD TRIP

Now that you have a basic understanding about minerals and the geological process that produce and concentrate them, it is time to start planning a collecting trip. Be advised that beginners are often guilty of setting such high expectations that the outing will have no hope for success. They feel it is only necessary to purchase a guidebook, drive to the described site, and the ground will be littered with beautiful glistening specimens. That is simply not the case! Any location that has been known long enough to be mentioned in a guidebook has probably been visited by hundreds of earlier collectors. If there was, at one time, lots to be found on easily accessible surface areas, most would certainly have been picked up by now. If you want success, it is imperative you understand that the best specimens are usually difficult to find.

Another common snag faced by novices is their lack of knowledge related to the mineral(s) being sought, especially as found in the field where they are rough, unpolished and uncleaned. The guidebooks are filled with photographs illustrating perfectly formed and colorful specimens, but they have been thoroughly cleaned, trimmed and selected from the best of the best.

It is also important that you allow sufficient time to properly explore any locality. It takes time to get a "feel" for the place and to see what the rough minerals look like. It takes additional time to follow your hunches and investigate promising areas.

It is sad to consider the number of ill-prepared beginners who became discouraged and disenchanted on their very first trips. So many have returned home to never try again, blaming the guidebook for sending them to unreliable locations. The sad part is that they probably hiked through areas that could have been productive had they spent some time doing a little advance planning and study.

Follow the guidelines provided within these covers and you should be able to gather enough to make any properly researched journey worthwhile. Do some reading about the region you plan to visit, know about the minerals you will search for, try to talk to someone who has already been there . . . research . . . research . . . research!

□ GUIDEBOOKS

If you go to a known mineral-producing location, you will have the greatest chance of finding something worthwhile. For that reason, it is recommended that you purchase one or more of the many field trip guidebooks on the market. Most cover a specific state or region and list exact locations known to supply good mineral specimens in worthwhile quantities. Now, that isn't to say you will never find something worthwhile by following your intuition, but, until you become more experienced, that "intuition" simply has no foundation.

A partial listing of guidebooks is in Appendix E, and you should have success with any of them. Just be sure to carefully read the descriptions, warnings, and road logs. The book(s) should provide collecting status information but, always remember, that such status is subject to change. A location that was open to collectors when the book was researched, may no longer be open when you visit.

PHOTO 15 *A selection of field trip guidebooks.*

Be sure the maps provide detailed mileage and the accompanying text has some hints related to gathering the minerals found at each listed site. Some books describe general and often widespread regions, rather than pinpointing particularly productive places, and thereby have little use to beginners.

Photographs are also helpful, especially if they depict minerals found at the site, a general view of the collecting area, or show collecting techniques particularly applicable to the location being described. Books with maps lacking detailed mileage, or featuring long and wordy site descriptions, filled with rambling generalities, or reports on places unavailable to collectors, create confusion and are often too cumbersome to be of practical use in the field. They might provide interesting information, but your primary field guide should be concise and to the point. It should be something you can take along for ready reference without having to weed your way through page after page of words not relevant to the practical task of actually finding minerals.

□ SUBSCRIPTIONS

There are many fine mineral and fossil magazines available and they often contain detailed and well-written field trip articles. Some of the most popular are listed in the bibliography, and you might consider subscribing to one or more of them. That way you will be provided with up-to-date information on a regular basis. Major book stores, gem shows, as well as rock and lapidary shops, usually have a variety of magazines and journals for sale and it is there where you can page through samples.

One difficulty with magazines is in trying to remember which sites are described in which issues. To overcome that disadvantage, it is suggested that you either maintain an index of articles, or, if you do not mind tearing them up, establish a file system where folders can be used to hold field trip information from a specific state or region. With such a filing system, if you are planning a trip to Arizona, for example, just take out the Arizona folder and there you have all the articles discussing collecting sites in Arizona. That information, accompanied by a good guidebook, will provide lots of ideas.

□ MINERAL REFERENCE BOOKS

In addition to field trip books, there are countless mineralogy, geology, and fossil volumes available, all capable of increasing your knowledge base. Remember, the more you know about what you are looking for, the better your chances of finding the best specimens.

You should also consider purchasing an easy-to-read book on mineral identification. It can be used as a supplement to Chapter 4 and will provide even more tests and observations to assist with identification of not only the minerals described in Chapter 5, but countless others.

□ PRIVATE ORGANIZATIONS

Great sources of information for trips into new and unfamiliar territory include automobile clubs and chambers of commerce. They often have maps, camping and lodging information, recreational facility updates, and, occasionally, even rock and mineral collecting ideas.

⬜ MUSEUMS

Museums are excellent sources of mineral information, primarily affording an opportunity to view actual specimens. Any given mineral is much easier to spot in the field, if you know what it looks like. Many museums also conduct lectures related to minerals and collecting sites, and/or actually conduct field trips, sometimes making arrangements to access places otherwise closed to the public.

⬜ ROCK SHOPS & MINERAL DEALERS

Great sources for up-to-date collecting information are rock or lapidary shops in or near the region being visited. Make a few stops when in the area, not only for collecting advice, but also to have an opportunity to view local specimens. Rock and mineral shops are generally listed under "lapidary" or "rock shops" in the yellow pages of a phone book. Those working at such shops will probably be able to give you ideas about what the nearby region has to offer, what is open, and where and how to get permission to collect, if required.

A word of caution when asking for collecting information at rock shops is probably needed at this point. Gemstones, minerals, and nice fossils frequently create symptoms very similar to "gold fever." There is sometimes a justifiable fear that the very best or most productive locations may become depleted if word gets out. Getting accurate information from some shop owners, especially if they sell what you are looking for, might require some carefully phrased questioning. If you have a guidebook and/or recent articles describing a nearby location, all you might be able to accomplish at a rock shop is to see exactly what the local minerals look like.

Please do not misunderstand. Many shop owners will not only direct you to good collecting locations, they may even volunteer to take you there. Don't count on that, but it does happen from time to time. Some people thoroughly enjoy sharing information, while others want to keep it a secret.

⬜ CLUBS & ORGANIZATIONS

Try to join a mineral or lapidary club. Nothing is more helpful than first-hand information, and, in conjunction with club functions, you will have an opportunity to meet and talk with others who can give advice and suggestions. In addition, most clubs conduct field trips, and it is amazing how much you can learn by going on just a few such outings. Many clubs even offer formal instruction on mineralogy, mineral identification, and all aspects of lapidary and jewelry crafts. Reading about something cannot compare with actually seeing it done or being personally instructed.

Consider also contacting clubs in any region you plan to visit. Addresses and contact persons are generally available in mineral or lapidary magazines or even in the phone book.

□ GOVERNMENT AGENCIES

Just about every state has a department governing mining or mineral resources, and they can be a storehouse of useful information. A list of many such agencies is included in Appendix C. Simply write and request a publications list.

Many of the governmental agencies also publish information related to current and past mining within the state, and such data can provide good leads for collecting trips. You might get addresses for mining operations known for good mineral specimens and be able to make arrangements for collecting on an inactive dump or at a time when the mine is not being worked.

□ MAPS

Supplementary maps are essential if you plan to search for minerals in remote regions. Not only can they provide good collecting clues, but they can be lifesavers if you get lost. The three most useful types of supplementary maps are topographic, geological, and forest service, each of which will be discussed in more detail.

Topographic Maps

Topographic maps are very detailed in regard to the relative elevations of the land. Mountains, hills, canyons, lakes, streams, roads and valleys are depicted by the use of elevation or contour lines. Man-made features such as mines, roads, quarries, dams and buildings are also noted. They can be used to ascertain the relative ruggedness of terrain and can be lifesavers if lost, since prominent landmarks, including buttes, mountains, and canyons are easy to pick out. They are very useful for orienting yourself, pinpointing exact locations and, if necessary, plotting a way out.

Probably the most useful feature of a topographic map is the way in which it depicts steepness of hills or canyons. This is done by the use of contour lines, which connect all features at a particular elevation. So, for example, a 5000 contour line will connect all points at 5000 feet above sea level. If the contour lines are far apart, then the terrain represented on the map is somewhat flat. If, however, the lines are very close together, then the terrain is steep.

The two most useful types are those depicting 15 minutes of latitude and, if even more detail is desired, those covering 7 minutes of latitude. The 7-minute maps show about one mile on the ground for every two inches on the map, and the 15-minute maps cover about one mile for every inch on the map. Topographic maps are published by the U.S. Geological Survey. Index maps for all states east of the Mississippi River can be ordered by writing to the Map Distribution Center, U.S. Geological Survey, 1200 South Eads Street, Arlington, VA 22202. For maps covering states west of the Mississippi River, write to the Map Distribution Center, U.S. Geological Survey, Federal Center, Box 25286, Denver, CO 80225.

Geologic Maps

Geologic maps show the various rock types and their approximate age. They provide information about the underlying rock, situated directly below the surface soil and foliage and most also illustrate land features such as rivers, valleys, canyons and mountains, but not with the detail supplied on topographic maps. The different rock types are easy to sort out, since each has its own specific color and/or pattern.

Again, geologic maps are interesting, but they do have limited practicality for hobby collectors. They provide no indication of how deep the overlying soil is and thereby only furnish clues to barren, fully exposed bedrock. Geologic maps can be purchased from state geological departments and mining associations, or occasionally through museums or geology departments at major colleges and universities. Some sources are listed in the bibliography.

For the advanced collector, geologic maps can be useful, especially if trying to locate new and yet undiscovered mineral deposits. If you know a specific mineral occurs within a particular geological setting, a geologic map will help you locate similar nearby situations.

Forest Service Maps

Forest service maps are very useful for collecting expeditions within national forests. They are probably the best maps for illustrating backroads, four-wheel drive trails, campgrounds, rivers, and other major landmarks. They are not as detailed as topographic maps, and land features are a little tougher to sort out, but they are easy to read and even provide road and trail numbers. They can be obtained at any forest service office in or near the region you will be exploring or by sending payment to the local forest service station or a regional distribution center. For some addresses, see Appendix C.

□ CONCLUSION

After all the discussion of guidebooks, clubs, museums, maps, classes, supplementary books, etc., the best assurance for a successful collecting trip is experience. As you take more and more field trips, there will begin to be things that seem familiar, thereby helping direct you to the most productive spots. Each trip will tend to afford you with more success and it is imperative you don't get discouraged on your first few outings. Just like so many other things, it takes practice to enhance your skills.

Chapter 3: Tools For Collecting

It is important to remind you that no matter how much potential a particular site seems to have, the minerals will probably not just be lying on the ground waiting to be picked up. It is normally necessary to expend some energy and use some specialized tools to get the best material a given spot has to offer.

This chapter deals with some of the most basic tools available to amateur mineral collectors. Armed with this equipment, a beginner can greatly enhance the chances of finding better specimens. The tools and other items discussed in the next few pages can be purchased from most lapidary and rock shops, and, in some cases, even hardware stores. If you have trouble finding what you need, obtain any rock, mineral or lapidary magazine for advertisements placed by dealers and manufacturers.

Suggestions for how to use the field collecting equipment discussed in this chapter are presented in Chapter 7. Apparatus required for cutting and polishing gemstones or for making jewelry will be described in Chapters 11 and 12.

□ THE ESSENTIALS

Hammers

Probably the one piece of equipment most identified with rockhounding and prospecting is the hand held rock pick (Photo 16). Generally, one side of the head is blunt and flat, while the opposite is either pointed or chisel shaped. If there is only one tool you can take on a field trip, this surely would be the most useful for most situations. The flattened end is handy for cracking small rocks and driving chisels or gads into seams or cracks. The pointed or flattened end is good for light digging or for prying open cracks.

A sledge hammer is extremely helpful if you need to break up sizable pieces of rock or are trying to extract gems still encased in seams or cavities. It is much heavier than a standard rock pick and far more effective for breaking up boulders and tough rocks. A sledge hammer also supplies more power for pounding chisels or gads into hard rock, or for breaking off samples from an outcrop. Sledge hammers come in a variety of weights and are available with short or long handles. Those with short handles are the most popular, since they are much easier to carry in the field and can be used with more precision. Sometimes, however, more weight and leverage is necessary. In those cases, a long-handled sledge is preferable.

Keep in mind, however, that sledge hammers are capable of doing considerable damage to gemstones and crystals if not used with care. Many beautiful specimens have been totally destroyed by their careless use. It would be much better to spend more time with a lightweight hand sledge or rock pick to open a cavity or seam than to pulverize everything with a huge sledge hammer.

PHOTO 16 *Two rock picks on either side of a short-handled, hand sledge hammer.*

One word of caution is necessary in regard to purchasing hammers for use on rock. Be sure you get one designed for such an application. Standard hammers will flake and splinter, thereby presenting a potentially hazardous situation.

Rock Chisels, Gads, and Star Drills

A rock chisel is a hand tool, with a sharpened flat end, used to trim specimens, chip off samples, or to split rocks and seams. A gad is a similar hand tool, but, instead of having a flat end, it is pointed. Gads are primarily used to break up rock or are inserted in cracks or seams to split them open. Gads are more useful to rockhounds, since their pointed and tapered ends tend to get

farther inside cracks and crevices than chisels. A star drill looks much like a gad, but it is thinner and primarily used to make holes in rock within which a gad can be inserted to do its job.

PHOTO 17 *(Left to right) A gad, small chisel, medium chisel, and star.*

26

Gads, chisels, and star drills can be purchased in a variety of widths, lengths and weights. As was the case with hammers, be certain to obtain only those designed for use on rock. Otherwise, dangerous splintering or breakage might occur.

Trowel

A trowel is a small hand-held digging tool which is very helpful when exploring mine dumps, washes, or regions where light digging of soft surface soil is required. Other small garden tools such as hand rakes can also be helpful in such situations.

PHOTO 18 *(Left to right) A pry bar, hand trowel, hand rake, and hand trowel.*

Pry Bar

Pry bars often come in handy when working hard rock seams or cavities. Furthermore, they can be used to break up tough soil and move large boulders. Pry bars afford better leverage than smaller hand tools and are much stronger, thereby being less likely to bend or break.

Pick and Shovel

Picks and shovels are needed when you must dig to locate minerals. At many sites, the surface material has all been taken, but, not too far below, there are still lots of excellent specimens. Getting to those otherwise hidden stones is made possible by using a pick and shovel.

If you need to hike to a mineral deposit, portable, folding shovels and picks (Photo 19) can be purchased, but the non-collapsible versions tend to be the most sturdy and efficient. A round ended shovel is the best for digging, while the most efficient pick is a mattock. One side of a mattock's digging end is pointed and the opposite side is flat and chisel-like. A mattock pick is capable of doing all kinds of digging, from precise trenching to large scale dirt moving. The pointed end offers excellent penetration, especially if working in hard soil, and, once the soil is loosened, the chisel end is great for removing dirt quickly.

Safety Goggles

Safety goggles (Photo 19) are a must when doing any hammering onto hard rock. Rock fragments or splintered metal from your hammer can fly off at the speed of a bullet when struck, thereby creating a potentially hazardous situation. It is tempting to "carefully" strike rocks with a hammer, but even the most perfect placement can inadvertently cause a razor sharp fragment to shoot through the air in an unplanned direction. The minor inconvenience of wearing goggles, is nothing compared to the potential consequences if they are not worn.

Hat and Proper Clothing

Taking clothing appropriate to the location(s) you will be visiting is essential if you want the trip to be an enjoyable experience. Be prepared for just about anything. Rain, mud, extremely hot weather, extremely cold weather, and even insects. Mineral deposits don't seem to ever be near clothing or convenience stores. In fact, most are not near much of anything, so prepare for the worst. It is much better to have more than you need, and not require it, rather than need it and not have it! As was mentioned in Chapter 2, do some research on the region you plan to visit. Will you be in the barren and desolate desert or rugged mountains? Should you expect snow or rain, or will it be scorching hot? Keep in mind that deserts can get very cold in the winter and high mountains can get hot in the summer.

PHOTO 19 *(Left to right) A hand winch, collapsible pick, flashlight (for seeing inside cavities or seams), hard hat, long handled probe for reaching into cavities or seams, goggles and boots for wading.*

If heading to the desert, a hat can shade your face from the extreme intensity of the sun and might prevent the trip from being miserable. A heavy jacket could be the difference between being able to collect or having to return home if the weather gets too cold.

Footwear is also of prime importance. Wear shoes appropriate to the terrain you will be exploring. If going to wet areas, waterproof shoes would be nice, as would an extra dry pair. If in hot and arid regions, shoes that "breathe" should be considered.

28

Gloves

If you plan to do anything except pick up specimens from the surface, gloves are recommended. Using a rock pick or sledge hammer for a few hours, or digging with pick and shovel, can cause painful blisters, cuts, and abrasions on one's hands. The associated tenderness and pain can quickly take the joy out of a collecting expedition. A good pair of gloves can make such handicaps less likely.

Collecting Bag or Backpack

When you visit a collecting site, it will probably be necessary to do some walking from where you park, and it is surprising how far you might stray. There is a limit to how much a person can carry in their pockets and hands, however, and that limit seems to always be reached just before coming upon the most beautiful specimen of your hike.

A sturdy bag or backpack made from canvas or rip-stop nylon comes in quite handy in situations like this. There is still a limit to how much a collecting bag or backpack can hold, but it is considerably more than your hands and pockets, and far more convenient.

□ ADDITIONAL SUGGESTED EQUIPMENT

Hard Hat

You probably think that a hard hat (Photo 19) is only for full-scale miners. That isn't true, however. If you are collecting near or on a steep cliff or quarry wall, a hard hat can serve as protection from whatever may be dislodged from higher up. If others are working above you, they could inadvertently loosen a rock and a hard hat might prevent a serious injury. Always wear a hard hat when working in a place where rock or other objects have even the slightest possibility of falling on your head. Hard hats come in all sizes and strengths. Be sure to get one of good quality, since it will last for years.

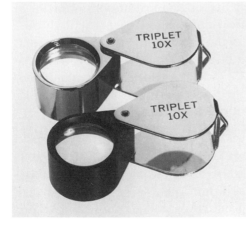

Loupe

A loupe is a small, pocket magnifier that folds into an attached protective shield (Photo 20). Loupes can assist with mineral identification and determining a particular gem's quality. You can better see identifying characteristics by magnification, especially if the specimen is small. While not essential in the field, a magnifier can certainly add interest to the trip.

PHOTO 20 *Loupes to use in the field.*

Screwdrivers

Flat screwdrivers can be helpful in some situations. Mineral-bearing cavities are often filled with soil or clay, and a screwdriver can clean them out. In addition, they can be used as probes or for removing dirt and clay from minerals once they have been recovered. Do not use screwdrivers as wedges or for pounding, since they are easily broken and are not designed to serve as substitutes for gads, chisels or star drills.

Rags

Rags have many field applications. They are excellent for cleaning hands, clothing and even specimens. Equally as important, they are invaluable when used to protect delicate minerals from damage while being transported home. Rags can also be stuffed into cavities or seams to protect included crystals from breakage while trying to free them.

Wrapping Materials

In addition to rags, newspaper, tissue paper, plastic "bubbles," styrofoam pellets, and even sawdust can be used to protect fragile specimens from being damaged while being transported back home. Newspapers are the easiest and least expensive wrapping and cushioning material available, but sometimes the ink rubs off. If you want to use newspaper, be sure to first cover specimens with an inner layer of something else.

Zip-Lock Bags

Zip-lock bags are handy for storing and collecting small gemstones. They can be securely sealed to prevent specimens from falling out, they are relatively easy to keep track of, they are watertight, and they are transparent, so you can see what is inside.

Pens/Pencils and a Notebook

Pencils or pens are nice to have along for many reasons. As mentioned in the last chapter, experience is probably the single most important factor in ensuring successful collecting. If you take notes related to a particularly productive area regarding the appearance of the surrounding terrain, associated minerals, color of soil, texture of soil and surrounding rock, etc. it will force you to be more aware of the often subtle indicators designating mineral occurrences. Even if you don't ever read the notes again, just the act of writing this information forces you to become more aware of the surroundings.

Camera and Extra Film

Taking a camera can serve many purposes. First, many of your expeditions will take you into extremely scenic areas and it would be a shame not to have a camera on hand to record it. In addition, a camera can be used to take photos of the region near a particularly productive mineral deposit or to record specific mineral-bearing situations. By making photographic records of your trips, subsequent journeys into similar settings may be more successful.

Sifting Screen

If you plan to work in a sand/gravel area or on a mine dump, a sturdy screening device is very helpful for use in separating the soil and pebbles. To use a sifting screen, you simply shovel mineral- bearing soil into it and sift out the finer material by shaking. Larger rocks will be trapped inside so they can be carefully inspected and those of interest retained.

PHOTO 21 *A homemade screening box.*

Sifting screens can be purchased from mining supply stores and some rock shops. If you want to make your own, first build a strong frame and then tightly attach a heavy screen with an approximate one-quarter inch mesh. If the screen is too fine, nothing much will be sifted out and if too coarse, you might lose what you are looking for.

Black Light

A black light is a device that emits ultraviolet light. When the ultraviolet rays come in contact with certain minerals in darkened surroundings, the results can be dramatic. Bright, vivid colors are often emitted, some of which are spectacular. This phenomena is referred to as fluorescence. Most minerals do not fluoresce, but those that do have potential for producing quite a show.

Black lights are generally hand held and battery powered so they can be taken into the field. If you are going to a region where there might be fluorescent minerals, a black light will be needed to find them. This is one of the few instances where nighttime collecting is not only possible, but essential. It is amazing how some of the most uninteresting stones will glow brilliant orange, yellow, green, blue, purple, red, or any other color of the rainbow when exposed to a black light.

PHOTO 22 *An ultraviolet light (black light). Courtesy of Raytech Industries Inc.*

31

If you do go black light collecting, be careful in the darkness and don't wander too far from your vehicle, since it might be tough to find your way back. Also keep in mind that some insects, including desert scorpions, fluoresce, so be careful!

Metal Detector

A metal detector is an electronic device that, through the process of generating an electromagnetic field, can detect the presence of metallic objects, including gold, silver and other such minerals and associated ores. There are all types on the market, and it can be quite confusing trying to determine which is the most suitable for your needs.

There are Pulse Induction detectors (PI), Beat Frequency Oscillators (BFO), as well as Phase Readout Gradiometers (PRG) and Two-Box Radio Frequency (RF) types. All will detect metal, but each has its limitations. Highly mineralized ground can make many of them worthless and, as you probably suspect, most minerals sought by metal detectors are generally found in places where the ground is quite mineralized. The most productive variety of detector for use in seeking gold and other metallic minerals seems to be the VLF/TR (Very Low Frequency Transmitter Receiver), since such devices can be tuned to partially overcome the effects of mineralized ground. They also penetrate considerably deeper than most others, and can discriminate between highly conductive metals, such as gold and silver and those that are less conductive, such as less valuable iron ores.

PHOTO 23 *A metal detector. Courtesy of White's Electronics.*

Gold Pans

Since many gemstone sites visited by collectors are also in areas noted for gold production, you might want to try your luck at panning. Nowadays there are a variety of pans from which to choose, including traditional steel and the newer plastic types. Each has its advantages and disadvantages. The plastic is lighter, won't corrode, and can be manufactured in a variety of shapes, but the steel pans can be used for heating items and are more durable.

Metal pans are usually shipped with a thin coating of oil to prevent rust. This oil, however, will cause gold and other minerals to slide out, so it must first be burned off. To do this, heat the pan very hot and then dip it in water. The oil will be removed and the pan will have a deep bluish-black color. This is called "bluing" and, in addition to removing the oil, it makes the gold easier to spot, because of its darker color.

Winch

A hand winch (see Photo 19) is a device used for moving heavy objects such as large boulders and fallen trees. They are not too expensive, and can also be helpful in getting your vehicle out of unpleasant situations. A good hand winch can be used to free a stuck car from deep sand or slick mud. If you are going into rugged or desolate country, a winch might be one of the best security investments you can make.

First-Aid Kit

Nobody goes into the wilderness or off the major roads thinking they may be hurt, but it happens from time to time. Most injuries sustained by rockhounds consist of small cuts and bruises, requiring no more than a Band-Aid, but you should still be prepared.

In addition, many favorite mineral collecting regions are also favorite hide-outs for rattlesnakes, venomous insects and spiders. Do some research about the place(s) you plan to visit. Know if there are poisonous insects or plants in the area and, if so, familiarize yourself about what they look like and where they will usually be encountered.

Car Repair Tools

Take along some of the basic car repair tools and make sure your spare tire is fully inflated. Dust and mud can get into places that cause problems and the constant vibration of travel on dirt roads can loosen parts such as battery cables, hoses, and wires. Most standard passenger cars are not designed for off-road travel, but, if that is your only source of transportation, use extreme caution and good judgment as to where you go. Even if you have a well-maintained, rugged, four-wheel drive vehicle, anything can happen. Take basic repair tools and a small tire inflator, and know how to use them!

Water and Snacks

No matter where you plan to search for minerals, it is recommended that you take along plenty of snacks and lots to drink. It never fails that just as you find a beautiful, crystal-filled cavity or a highly productive mineral deposit, you get deliriously thirsty or weak from lack of food. Furthermore, in case you get yourself stuck, the extra food and drink might become essential.

□ CONCLUSION

This concludes our brief look at some of the basic tools you might consider taking with you on a field trip. More tips on their use are provided in Chapter 7.

There are countless additional devices on the market that can be of great help in certain situations. They include spiral sluices, concentrators, shakers, specialized power supplies, rock drills, coring devices, as well as tractors, back hoes, bulldozers, jigs, underwater and surface dredges, and the list goes on and on. It is important to note, though, that no matter how sophisticated and expensive your equipment might be, there must be minerals present, in a worthwhile quantity. You can be in a low production area with all the equipment in the world and, if there isn't much to be found, it won't be of much use. That goes back to the essence of Chapter 2 - do some research related to the area you plan to visit before taking a field trip.

4 IDENTIFYING MINERALS

CHAPTER

Mineral identification is fun, something like solving a puzzle after being given a series of clues. Specialized equipment and thorough training in gemstone and mineral identification might be required in order to accurately determine the true identity of many specimens, but the commonly encountered materials discussed in this book tend to be relatively easy to identify.

When in the field, there are certain things you can look for to help determine exactly what you may have picked up. Such observations are not always conclusive, but, in many cases, they help with making educated guesses. This is particularly true if collecting in a region where specific minerals are known to occur in significant quantities. That is what often happens with beginners, since they are usually directed to locations by guidebooks or magazine articles, and the accompanying text will list the predominant minerals to be found there. All that must be done is to sort what has been found from a relatively small list of possibilities.

In the following paragraphs are eight simple tests and observations that will allow you to make educated guesses in regard to a mineral's identity. After conducting each of the tests, refer to the information provided in Chapter 5, Appendix B, or a mineral identification handbook, to systematically narrow down your list of possibilities. With experience, you will probably develop an ability to simply look at some of the more common minerals and quickly tell what they are.

(1) Appearance

Although general appearance is not a very precise or scientific test, it is probably the best means of identifying the most commonly encountered minerals. If it "looks like a quartz crystal," based upon previous observations of quartz crystals, then it might very well be a quartz crystal. In fact, the appearance of many commonly encountered minerals is so distinctive that any additional testing may be unnecessary. Little black, glass-like pebbles are probably Apache tears, chances are high that bright blue and green stains on native rock are either malachite or chrysocolla. Experience and previous observations of common minerals often makes them very easy to identify, especially when they exhibit distinctive characteristics.

(2) Hardness

Another fairly simple test used to help identify minerals involves determining hardness. Hardness is a mineral's resistance to being scratched. Harder minerals will scratch softer minerals. The commonly used reference is the ten step Mohs Scale. A hardness of 1 on that scale represents the softest or most easily scratched of minerals, while 10 is the hardest and most resistant to scratching. The following are minerals representing each level of the Mohs Scale.

(1) Talc	(6) Orthoclase
(2) Gypsum	(7) Quartz
(3) Calcite	(8) Topaz
(4) Fluorite	(9) Corundum
(5) Apatite	(10) Diamond

You can purchase a simple hardness test kit from lapidary or mining supply stores, but, for approximate estimates, the following references may be used: The hardness of a fingernail is about 2.5; a copper penny is 3.0; a pocket knife is 5.0; glass is 5.5; and a steel file rates a hardness of 6.5.

To test a mineral's hardness, try to scratch it on a clean and relatively smooth surface with any of the above items. The use of a magnifying glass is helpful in determining whether or not the mineral has actually been scratched. Be very careful not to be fooled by residue left on the specimen by the "scratching" material. Always clean off the surface before determining if it was actually penetrated. If no scratch occurs, try the next harder object until you get one, thereby allowing for an educated hardness estimate.

(3) Specific Gravity

Specific gravity is an attempt to describe a mineral's weight. What it is, in scientific terms, is the weight of a particular mineral compared to exactly the same volume of water. Precise determination of specific gravity, especially in the field, is very difficult and impractical. But, as part of the narrowing down process in a mineral's identification, if it "feels" heavy, then it has a high specific gravity. On the other hand, if it "feels" light, it has a low specific gravity. Granted, such a subjective test isn't very accurate, but, in the case of very heavy or very light materials, it can provide usable information when taken together with other tests.

(4) Streak

Even though different specimens of a given mineral may manifest many different colors, the powdered state tends to always be a consistent hue. The easiest way to determine the associated powder's color is to conduct what is called a streak test. This is accomplished by rubbing the mineral in question along a piece of white, rough, unglazed porcelain, or something similar. Examine the powder residue, or streak, and carefully determine its color, possibly with the aid of a loupe. Then refer to the information in Chapter 5 or a mineral identification book to verify which minerals may exhibit similarly colored streaks.

(5) Luster

The luster of a mineral is the way light is reflected off a clean and undamaged surface. The phrases used to describe luster are not overly precise, but are somewhat self-explanatory. Luster is described by such terms as metallic, submetallic and nonmetallic. Metallic is the most reflective and nonmetallic is the least reflective. Within the category of nonmetallic minerals are additional descriptive terms such as vitreous (glass-like), adamantine (diamond-like), resinous, earthy, dull, greasy, waxy, silky, and pearly (see glossary for definitions). When trying to get an accurate estimate of luster, it is necessary to break off a clean and fresh surface, since luster can be greatly altered by tarnish, oxidation, soil and abrasion.

(6) Fracture

Some minerals leave a characteristic pattern when broken, and such a condition is referred to as its fracture. To see how a mineral fractures, break off a portion and carefully look at the resulting surface. Sometimes a hand loupe will help with this inspection. The description of a fracture is usually provided by such terms as conchoidal, uneven, irregular, or fibrous, and definitions are provided in the glossary.

(7) Color

The color is helpful when trying to establish a mineral's identity, but definitely not as reliable as some of the other tests. Due to the often severe situations within which minerals crystallize or concentrate, as described in Chapter 1, it is unrealistic to think that pure forms are frequently found. There is almost always an infusion of some impurities, and often those impurities will alter, sometimes radically, the color of a particular specimen. Color, however, is usually one of the first things a collector will notice, and it does offer some clues. Color, when taken into consideration with other identification tests, is therefore helpful.

(8) Habit

Habit is very similar to appearance. It refers to the form (or one of the forms) that a specific mineral is known to possess. It is how the mineral usually appears in nature. Does it crystallize or is it massive? Does it look bubbly, layered, fibrous, smooth or flaky? Some of the terms used to describe habit are prismatic, pyramidal, botryoidal, mammillary, cubic, dendritic, rhombohedral, radiating, stalactitic, and bladed (see glossary for definitions). The habit of a particular mineral is often a very good clue to its identity.

CRYSTAL SYSTEMS

CUBE	**OCTAHEDRON**	**DODECAHEDRON**

ISOMETRIC

TRICLINIC	**MONOCLINIC**

PINACOIDS	**DIPYRAMID**	**PRISM**	**DIPYRAMID**

ORTHOROMBIC	**TETRAGONAL**

PRISM	**DIPYARAMID**	**RHOMBOHEDRON**

HEXAGONAL

Crystal structure is another reliable and consistent manifestation of habit, since most minerals, if allowed to form in unobstructed environments, which is somewhat rare, will crystallize in one of six general ways. The crystals of a specific mineral, due to its internal atomic structure, will always possess the same angles between faces, no matter how distorted. If those angles, faces, and its structure can be determined, which is sometimes very difficult, a prime key to identification is provided. The six basic categories of crystallization are triclinic, monoclinic, orthorhombic, tetragonal, hexagonal, and isometric (definitions are provided in the glossary).

It is very important to note, at this point, that many minerals can exhibit more than one habit, even at the same location. To further confuse the issue, occasionally, a given mineral may have gone through some sort of alteration and might possess the habit of another, totally unrelated mineral. Such interesting specimens are referred to as pseudomorphs and help to emphasize the need to conduct more than one test to accurately determine a mineral's true identity.

▢ WHERE TO GO FROM HERE

Since you will probably be visiting known locations described in field trip books or magazine articles, you should already know what collectable minerals can be found at a given site. That fact, alone, will greatly help you determine the identity of anything encountered. Furthermore, most such books provide assistance related to where the minerals might be found within any given site.

When you want to confirm the identity of a particular mineral, the process involves narrowing down the possibilities. You should start by limiting the choices to minerals known to occur at the place where it was found. If your choices involve any of the minerals described in Chapter 5, refer first to "Most Useful Clues For Identification," which may be all you need to do. If still not sure what's what, start looking at some of the other attributes. Conduct one test at a time, as described in the previous pages, trying to confirm as many properties as possible. By following this procedure, you will be able to eliminate some possibilities and confirm others. Most likely you will not be able to verify all characteristics, but you can still narrow it down to one choice, if only considering minerals known to be found at that site.

Some of the properties are not as easily established as others, especially when in the field. Specific gravity is a test of heaviness, and sizable specimens are usually needed in order to get an idea of relative weight. Often such pieces are not obtainable. Crystal systems are also difficult to discern, since very few specimens actually show their proportions perfectly. The inherent distortions exhibited by most mineral crystals, and the numerous variations of the six basic crystal systems, routinely make such determination very difficult. If you are already fairly certain about a particular mineral's identity, however, the crystal structure might be helpful to verify your conclusion.

Be sure to also refer to the color photographs in Chapter 5, but keep in mind that they depict cleaned and trimmed specimens. In addition, many minerals exhibit numerous forms, some radically different from each other, and the photos do not represent all possible occurrences. That is why all information associated with any mineral is valuable. A photograph is just one clue in the process of identification and, if not used in conjunction with other tests and examinations, it can be very misleading.

A complete guide to mineral identification is far beyond the scope of this book. If interested in learning more than these basic techniques, refer to Appendix E for additional sources of information.

Now let's look at those minerals . . . . .

CHAPTER 5 | COMMONLY ENCOUNTERED MINERALS

Anyone would love to stumble upon a beautiful ruby, emerald, diamond or gold nugget, but the chances of such a discovery are unlikely. If such gemstones were easy to find, they wouldn't have such great value. There are, however, many nice minerals available to amateur collectors, and this chapter presents some of the most commonly encountered examples. The following vignettes provide specific characteristics which should help you find and identify each of the minerals if you follow the guidelines presented in Chapter 4.

□ AZURITE

Most Useful Clues For Identification: Azurite's brilliant blue color, its association with other brightly colored copper ores, and its effervescence in hydrochloric acid are the most reliable indicators. It can be transparent, translucent, and even opaque. It is brittle, and found most commonly with malachite. Azurite is usually encountered by amateurs in the form of crusts or earthy masses. When crystallized (which is rare), the crystals often form rosette-like clusters.

Hardness: 3.5 - 4.0 **Specific Gravity:** 3.8
Streak: Light blue **Fracture:** Conchoidal
Luster: Dull **Crystal System:** Monoclinic
Common Color(s): Light blue to almost black.

Other Minerals Frequently Found With Azurite: Malachite, limonite, kaolin, other copper ores, quartz, and/or chalcedony.

Where Found: Azurite is seldom found at a great depth, since it is a secondary, weathered, oxidized copper ore. Be on the lookout for bright blue and green stains on the native rocks. If you should spot fragments of azurite or other brightly colored copper ores in a wash, attempt locating the source by following the easily spotted pebbles upstream. Scan adjacent mountainsides and canyons for the bright greens and blues.

☐ BARITE

Most Useful Clues For Identification: Barite is best identified by its distinctive crystallization (even though it might be tightly packed), good cleavage, brittleness, and relatively heavy weight. It can be transparent, translucent, and even opaque. Barite occurs in many forms including distinct tabular crystals and small, sand-filled rosette concretions called desert roses. It is most frequently found as compact, poorly formed, intergrown crystal clusters.

Hardness: 3.0 - 3.5   **Specific Gravity:** 4.4
Streak: White   **Fracture:** Uneven
Luster: Glassy or pearly   **Crystal System:** Orthorhombic
Common Color(s): Light blue, colorless, light yellow, brown, reddish brown.

Other Minerals Frequently Found With Barite: Calcite, dolomite, fluorite, quartz, galena, siderite, pyrite, chalcopyrite, and sphalerite.

Where Found: Barite is most generally encountered in sedimentary rocks where it may be encased within concretions or found free in the form of little rosettes.

☐ BERYL

Most Useful Clues For Identification: Hardness and the often well-defined, six-sided crystals are the best field identification hints. Beryl can be transparent to translucent and the crystals are often striated parallel to their length. The color is generally not uniform throughout the crystal.

Hardness: 7.5 - 8.0   **Specific Gravity:** 2.6 - 2.9
Streak: White or colorless   **Fracture:** Conchoidal or uneven
Luster: Glassy   **Crystal System:** Hexagonal
Common Color(s): White, blue (aquamarine), green (emerald), yellow (golden beryl), pink (morganite).

Other Minerals Frequently Found With Beryl: Quartz, feldspar, tourmaline, mica, lepidolite, and spodumene.

Where Found: The finest specimens of beryl are usually found in weathered pegmatites.

Beryl Varieties:
    Emerald: Light to dark shades of green.
    Aquamarine: Blue to greenish blue variety.
    Golden Beryl: Beryl displaying a brownish yellow color.
    Morganite: Light purple-red hues.

□ BORNITE

Most Useful Clues For Identification: The best way to identify bornite is by its often colorful, iridescent tarnish. It is opaque and brittle and often referred to as "Peacock Ore."

Hardness: 3.0   **Specific Gravity:** 5.0
Streak: Grayish black   **Fracture:** Uneven or conchoidal
Luster: Metallic   **Crystal System:** Isometric (rare!)
Common Color(s): Bronze, but usually tarnished.

Other Minerals Frequently Found With Bornite: Other copper minerals like chalcocite, chalcopyrite, as well as pyrite, marcasite, and quartz.

Where Found: Bornite is most commonly found in copper ore veins, usually in association with other secondary copper minerals. It is occasionally in pegmatites and contact metamorphic zones.

□ CALCITE

Most Useful Clues For Identification: Calcite can usually be identified by its softness, distinct rhombohedral cleavage (breaks up into little box-like pieces), and its ability to bubble in cold dilute hydrochloric acid. Calcite can vary from transparent to opaque. It is brittle and found in a wide variety of forms, including tabular or prismatic crystals, little needles, stalactite drip-like formations, rhombohedrons, and fibrous or granular masses. The Iceland spar rhombohedral occurrence, if transparent, will show double refraction. It often fluoresces, sometimes a beautiful, brilliant red.

Hardness: 3.0   **Specific Gravity:** 2.7
Streak: White to grayish   **Fracture:** Conchoidal (hard to spot)
Luster: Glassy   **Crystal System:** Hexagonal
Common Color(s): Colorless, white, other pale hues, depends on impurities.

Other Minerals Frequently Found With Calcite: Just about all types of rocks and minerals can be found with calcite.

Where Found: Calcite is one of the most common minerals and can be found just about anywhere. It is the primary constituent of limestone and marble, and fine specimens are encountered in pegmatites and some hydrothermal regions. The massive banded variety is known as onyx, and can be used to make beautiful carvings, bookends, or cabochons.

□ CHALCEDONY (INCLUDING AGATE & JASPER)

Most Useful Clues For Identification: Chalcedony is best identified by its dull, waxy appearance, conchoidal fracture, and often beautiful colors. It can be semitransparent to translucent or even completely opaque. Chalcedony and crystalline quartz are chemically the same, but chalcedony is microscopically crystallized and usually contains impurities. The surface tends to be botryoidal (see glossary), and it is often smooth. The best formed bubbly pieces are referred to as chalcedony roses.

Hardness: 7.0   **Specific Gravity:** 2.6
Streak: White   **Fracture:** Conchoidal
Luster: Waxy or glassy   **Crystal System:** None
Common Color(s): Colorless, white, pink, blue, yellow, gold, red, brown.

Other Minerals Frequently Found With Chalcedony: Chalcedony is not necessarily found in association with other minerals, but it often contains crystals of such minerals as rutile, hornblende, tourmaline, actinolite, calcium, magnesium, or manganese. Such pieces, if the internally encased minerals are easily distinguished, can be very interesting.

Where Found: Chalcedony is usually found near igneous formations such as rhyolite, granite or basalt. Search throughout adjacent flatlands in or near these areas and also inspect washes leading downstream from such locations.

Agate
The banded translucent variety of chalcedony is called agate. Varieties are named according to their mode of banding, inclusions, and/or patterning.

Agate Varieties:
> *Fortification agate* - composed of straight intersecting bands.
> *Moss agate* - milky white and filled with black or brown fuzzy moss-like inclusions.
> *Dendritic agate* - semitransparent chalcedony with branching tree-like inclusions.
> *Plume agate* - agate with inclusions that look like plumes or flowers.
> *Sagenite* - agate filled with needle-like inclusions.
> *Banded agate* - material exhibiting gray, light blue, brown, red, or black curved bands.

Agatized Wood
This is more commonly referred to as petrified wood. Agatized wood is what results when ancient tree sections have been completely replaced with chalcedony. Some specimens are very beautiful and can contain a rainbow of colors, including red, yellow, blue, black and brown.

Bloodstone
Is a semitransparent to opaque dark-green chalcedony exhibiting red or brownish red spots and splotches.

Carnelian
Carnelian is a semitransparent or translucent red to orange-red variety of chalcedony.

Chert & Flint

Chert and flint usually don't have bands, are fairly opaque, and are often more grainy than other chalcedonies.

Chrysoprase

This is a highly desirable, semitransparent pale to apple-green chalcedony.

Geodes

These are hollow, orbicular shells containing layers of banded chalcedony and mineral crystals, usually calcite or quartz. If the shell is completely filled with agate, the deposit is called a nodule.

Jasper

The name jasper applies to most of the opaque or nearly opaque chalcedonies, which may show a wide variety of colors and patterns. Colors include red, yellow, brown, green, grayish blue, or any combination thereof. Like agate, it has many sub-varieties and generally the prefix is used for description such as red jasper, green jasper, banded jasper, and flower jasper.

▫ CHRYSOCOLLA

Most Useful Clues For Identification: Chrysocolla is best identified by its brilliant blue-green color. It is frequently found in an uncrystallized, massive state, as bubbly deposits, or stains on native rock. Solid material is often filled with black streaks and stringers. It is translucent to opaque and generally somewhat brittle.

Hardness: 2.0 - 4.0 **Specific Gravity:** 2.0 - 2.3
Streak: White **Fracture:** Conchoidal
Luster: Glassy or waxy **Crystal System:** Monoclinic
Common Color(s): Sky-blue to greenish blue and green, often streaked with black.

Other Minerals Frequently Found With Chrysocolla: Azurite, malachite, native copper, limonite, chalcedony, and quartz.

Where Found: Chrysocolla is found in surface regions of oxidized copper. Be on the lookout for the bright blue and green stains on the native rocks. This is an indication of copper content and usually designates the presence of chrysocolla. If you should spot traces in a wash, attempt locating the source. Scan adjacent mountainsides and canyons for the bright greens and blues.

▫ CORUNDUM

Most Useful Clues For Identification: Corundum is very hard, relatively heavy, and customarily found as distinctive, tabular, six-sided crystals with intersecting parallel striations. Sometimes these crystals look barrel-like. Specimens can range from transparent all the way to opaque. The six-sided crystallization of corundum resembles, and might be confused with, some of the feldspars.

Hardness: 9.0

Specific Gravity: 4.0

Streak: White

Fracture: Conchoidal or uneven

Luster: Glassy

Crystal System: Hexagonal

Common Color(s): Colorless, brown, black, yellow, red (ruby), blue, violet (non-red colors are sapphires).

Other Minerals Frequently Found With Corundum: Magnetite, hematite, spinel, tourmaline, mica, garnet, kyanite, and high calcium feldspars.

Where Found: Corundum is often found in metamorphised limestone, mica schists, and pegmatites. Due to its extreme hardness and density, it is also encountered in river gravels.

Corundum Varieties:

Ruby: This is the transparent, medium to dark red to purple-red variety of corundum. Very light tones of red should be referred to as pink sapphire.

Star Ruby: Ruby that displays a distinct star when cut as a cabochon.

Sapphire: The term sapphire refers to all colors of corundum other than the reds of ruby. Sapphire used alone means the blue variety, and all other hues are prefixed with the descriptive color, such as pink sapphire, yellow sapphire, etc.

Star sapphire: Any sapphire that shows a distinct star when cut as a cabochon.

☐ FELDSPAR

Feldspar is actually a family of minerals. For our purposes, as beginners, all will be grouped together. The major varieties of feldspar are orthoclase, microcline, and the plagioclase series.

Most Useful Clues For Identification: Feldspar is best identified by its crystallization (sometimes quite large), blocky cleavage, and hardness. It can range all the way from transparent to opaque and is generally quite brittle. Many crystals demonstrate an interesting phenomenon called twinning.

Hardness: 6.0 - 6.5

Specific Gravity: 2.5 - 2.7

Streak: White

Fracture: Uneven

Luster: Glassy or pearly

Crystal System: Monoclinic (orthoclase); Triclinic (microcline and plagioclase)

Common Color(s): White, yellow, reddish brown, black, brown, colorless, reddish, green.

Other Minerals Frequently Found With Feldspar: Orthoclase is associated with quartz and muscovite. Microclene is often found with quartz in pegmatites.

Where Found: Orthoclase is a very common rock-forming mineral and can be just about anywhere. Most commonly, orthoclase occurs in granites, pegmatites, and rhyolite. Microcline is found in hydrothermal veins, areas of contact metamorphism, and in pegmatites, where the crystallization can be sizable. Plagioclase is primarily in igneous and metamorphic rocks.

Feldspar Varieties:

Sanidine: Sanidine forms nice glassy tabular crystals inside cavities of some volcanic rock.

Moonstone: This is one of the more highly prized feldspars, noted for its shimmering bluish sheen (which is referred to as adularescence). It is most prized as a gem material.

Labradorite: A member of the plagioclase series, also of special interest to collectors. It rarely forms crystals, and exhibits a sometimes spectacular play of colors against a blue, gray, white, or colorless background.

Amazonite: A prized green and blue-green variety of microcline that often shows large and perfectly formed crystallization.

Cleavelandite: An interesting form of albite which crystallizes in thin blades.

□ FLUORITE

Most Useful Clues For Identification: Fluorite is best identified by its relative softness and nice cubic crystals, which are sometimes twinned. It can be semi-transparent to transparent, is somewhat brittle, and frequently breaks up into little cubes and/or octahedrons when struck. It also occurs as granular masses and often fluoresces.

Hardness: 4.0	**Specific Gravity:** 3.1
Streak: White	**Fracture:** Conchoidal or uneven
Luster: Glassy	**Crystal System:** Isometric

Common Color(s): Just about any color, including colorless, black, white, brown, blue, yellow, green, and violet.

Other Minerals Frequently Found With Fluorite: Calcite, dolomite, barite, quartz, galena, pyrite, chalcopyrite and sphalerite. Sometimes also wolframite, topaz, tourmaline, molybdenite, and apatite.

Where Found: Fluorite is often found in sedimentary rocks, hydrothermal ore veins, and in pegmatites. Outstanding crystals are sometimes encountered in sedimentary rock cavities.

□ GALENA

Most Useful Clues For Identification: Galena usually displays perfect cubic crystals and cleavage. Other indicators are its softness, lead-gray color, luster, and heavy weight. It is opaque, brittle, and the crystal faces are usually dull.

Hardness: 2.5 - 2.7 **Specific Gravity:** 7.4 - 7.6
Streak: Lead gray **Fracture:** Slight conchoidal
Luster: Metallic **Crystal System:** Isometric
Common Color(s): Lead gray

Other Minerals Frequently Found With Galena: Sphalerite, pyrite, chalcopyrite, quartz, siderite, dolomite, fluorite, calcite or barite.

Where Found: Galena is often found in metal ore veins, as well as within cavities and fissures of many types of igneous and sedimentary rocks.

▢ GARNET

Garnet is actually a family of minerals including almandite, andradite, pyrope, spessartine, uvarovite, and grossularite. At least one of the garnet group is found in just about every igneous and metamorphic type of rock. They might be microscopic constituents, or they could be sizable crystals.

Most Useful Clues For Identification: Garnet is usually best identified by its color and generally consistent crystallization. It can range from transparent to opaque, with most being semitransparent.

Hardness: 6.5 - 7.5 **Specific Gravity:** 3.4 - 4.3
Streak: White **Fracture:** Conchoidal
Luster: Glassy **Crystal System:** Isometric
Common Color(s): Brown, black, deep violet-red, slightly brownish red to purplish red, green, yellow-green, orange, pink, deep purple.

Other Minerals Frequently Found With Garnet: *Almandine* is usually associated with andalusite, kyanite, and staurolite. *Andradite* can occur in association with feldspar and biotite mica in granite pegmatites, as well as with calcite. *Grossularite* is often associated with calcite, epidote, and diopside. *Pyrope* is frequently found with serpentine, olivine, and spinel. *Spessertine* frequently occurs with mica and quartz. *Uvarovite* is commonly associated with chromite, olivine, and serpentine.

Where Found: *Almandine* is the most frequently encountered species of garnet. It is usually in metamorphic rocks, most frequently mica schist and gneiss. When in mica schists, it often exhibits beautifully faced crystals. *Andradite* commonly coats seams and crusts in igneous and metamorphic rocks, but does not occur in mica schists. One of the primary sources is in contact zones involving limestone and lava. *Grossularite* is usually in metamorphized limestones and contact zones. It can also form on seams or in pegmatite pockets, showing smooth crystal faces. *Pyrope* is usually encountered in igneous rocks, frequently with olivine. It also occurs in association with serpentine. *Spessartite* is frequently in rhyolite pockets, as well as in pegmatites and some types of metamorphic rock. *Uvarovite* oftentimes coats seams in chromite rich rock and is sometimes found in hydrothermal veins and metamorphic material.

□ GOLD

Most Useful Clues For Identification: Gold is identified by its bright golden yellow color, metallic luster, relatively heavy weight, and softness. It will not break when hit by a hammer, while pyrite and most other substances confused with gold will crumble. It is opaque and often found combined with silver. Gold often occurs in irregular masses called nuggets, and crystals are very rare. Keep in mind, when conducting tests on any suspected gold nuggets, that naturally occurring specimens can be quite valuable. If you do find a nice nugget, don't ruin it by pounding or scratching with a knife, rely only on less destructive tests.

Hardness: 2.5 - 3.0   **Specific Gravity:** 15.6 - 19.3
Streak: Golden yellow   **Fracture:** Hackly
Luster: Metallic   **Crystal System:** Isometric
Common Color(s): Gold and a rich yellow to silvery yellow.

Other Minerals Frequently Found With Gold: Quartz, pyrite, arsenopyrite, sphalerite, galena, and molybdenite.

Where Found: Gold is primarily found in hydrothermal quartz or sulfide veins. Since it does not readily combine with other minerals and because it is quite durable and heavy, it is frequently able to concentrate in stream beds, either as flakes or in larger nuggets.

□ GYPSUM

Most Useful Clues For Identification: The best way to identify gypsum is by its softness. It is actually so soft that it can be scratched with a fingernail. It varies from transparent to opaque and beautiful bladed crystals are not uncommon. It also occurs in massive, granular and fibrous states.

Hardness: 1.5 - 2.0   **Specific Gravity:** 2.3
Streak: White   **Fracture:** Conchoidal or splintery
Luster: Glassy, pearly, silky
Crystal System: Monoclinic
Common Color(s): Colorless, white, and light tints (due to impurities).

Other Minerals Frequently Found With Gypsum: Halite, barite, dolomite, sulfur, aragonite, and quartz.

Where Found: Gypsum is most often found in sedimentary rocks or within limestone cavities. Large bedded sedimentary deposits, such as ancient sea beds, sandstone or shale, are excellent spots to look for gypsum. Gypsum can also occasionally be found in hydrothermal regions.

Gypsum Varieties:
   Alabaster is the massive occurrence.
   Satin spar is a fibrous variety.

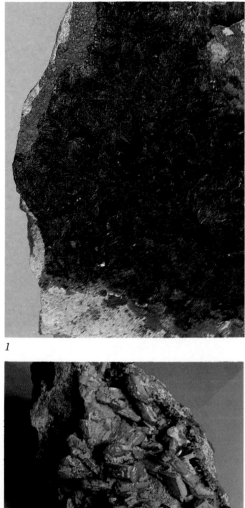

1

2

3

¹ *Rosette crystals of azurite*
² *Polished azurite with limonite*
³ *Azurite balls with malachite*
⁴ *Golden barite crystals*
⁵ *Barite balls*
⁶ *Beryl (aquamarine) crystal in quartz*

4

5

6

49

7

8

9

10

7 *Bornite*
8 *Needle crystals of calcite*
9 *Onyx variety of calcite*
10 *Concretion filled with calcite crystals*
11 *Rhombohedral calcite in sandstone*
12 *Chalcedony rose*
13 *Calcite crystals*

11

12

13

14

15

14 *Plume agate*
15 *Petrified wood*
16 *Red jasper*
17 *Lake Superior agate courtesy of
Michael Carlsen*
18 *Carnelian necklace*
19 *Polished agates and jaspers*

16

17

18

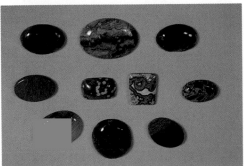

19

21

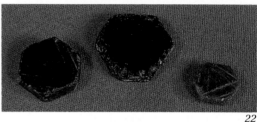

22

20 *Chrysocolla on tiny quartz crystals*
21 *Chrysocolla & malachite on limonite*
22 *Corundum (ruby)*
23 *Corundum (sapphire)*
24 *Feldspar (amazonite)*
25 & 26 *Flourite*

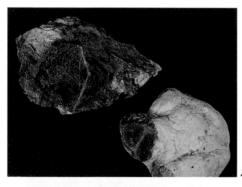

23

24

25

26

27

28

29

30

27 *Galena with quartz*   31 *Gold nuggets*
28 *Galena*   32 *Gypsum*
29 *Garnet crystals*   *(selenite crystals)*
30 *Garnet*   33 *Halite*

31

32

33

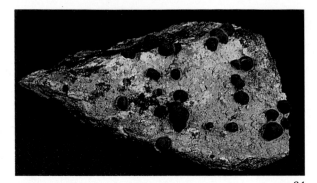

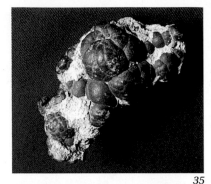

34

35

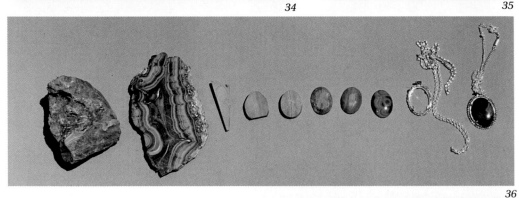

36

34 *Small balls of malachite*
35 *Botryoidal hematite*
36 *Malachite—from rough stone to finished necklace*
37 *Marble*
38 *Malachite and calcite on limonite*
39 *Mica and feldspar crystals*

37

39

38

40

41

40 *Obsidian*
41 *Precious opal*
42 *Common opal*
43 *Pyrite and siderite crystals*
44 *Large pyrite crystal with quartz*
45 *Herkimer diamonds*
46 *Quartz crystals*

42

43

44

45

46

47

48

49

50

51

52

53

[47] *Large flattened quartz crystals*
[48] *Geodes filled with chalcedony and quartz crystals*
[49] *Serpentine*
[50] *Tourmaline crystals*
[51] *Black tourmaline (schoral) with malachite and chrysocolla*
[52] *Wire silver*
[53] *Pink tourmaline crystals (rubellite) in lepidolite*

Gypsum Varieties (cont.):

> *Selenite* is the glassy, often crystallized form, thereby being the most prized form.
>
> *Sand selenite* is selenite which has crystallized within sand, thereby forming interesting, opaque, sand-filled clusters.

▫ HALITE

Most Useful Clues For Identification: Halite is identified by its cubic, sometimes hopper-like crystals, as well as a distinct cleavage. It is transparent, brittle, and very soluble in water. It also occasionally exhibits octahedral crystallization, but most commonly forms as masses or granular deposits on native rock.

Hardness: 2.0 - 2.5   **Specific Gravity:** 2.16
Streak: White   **Fracture:** Conchoidal
Luster: Glassy   **Crystal System:** Isometric
Common Color(s): Colorless, white, and sometimes reddish or blue from impurities.

Other Minerals Frequently Found With Halite: Other evaporate minerals such as gypsum, dolomite, and anhydrite.

Where Found: Halite is often found in dried lake beds in arid climates or on the shoreline of very salty lakes.

▫ HEMATITE

Most Useful Clues For Identification: One of the most decisive indicators of hematite is its distinctive brownish red streak. It is opaque and brittle, and the metallic tabular or bladed crystals are often beautiful, sometimes in the form of rosettes. Hematite also occurs in massive, fibrous, botryoidal, and granular states.

Hardness: 5.0 - 6.0   **Specific Gravity:** 4.9 - 5.3
Streak: Red   **Fracture:** Uneven or splintery
Luster: Metallic   **Crystal System:** Hexagonal
Common Color(s): Steel gray, red, silver, or black.

Other Minerals Frequently Found With Hematite: Magnetite, limonite, goethite, and chalcedony.

Where Found: Hematite is sometimes found in schist, regions of contact metamorphism, or in limestone pockets. It can also be found in iron rich soft, red earthy masses.

□ MALACHITE

Most Useful Clues For Identification: Malachite is best identified by its bright green color, as well as its botryoidal deposition. It can vary from translucent to opaque and is quite brittle. Malachite often forms as silky, rounded green masses, and even as stalactites and stalagmites, and rarely crystallizes.

Hardness: 3.5 - 4.0   **Specific Gravity:** 3.9
Streak: Light green   **Fracture:** Splintery or conchoidal
Luster: Glasslike, silky or dull   **Crystal System:** Monoclinic (rare!)
Common Color(s): Light to dark green

Other Minerals Frequently Found With Malachite: Limonite, azurite, cuprite chrysocolla, native copper, kaolin, quartz, and chalcedony.

Where Found: Malachite is the most common of the secondary copper ores, and is usually found near the surface. Be on the lookout for bright blue and green stains on the native rocks, since those are highly visible indicators of oxidized copper ores. If you should spot traces in a wash, attempt locating the source. Scan adjacent mountainsides and canyons for the bright greens and blues.

□ MARBLE

A ROCK TYPE (Not a Mineral)

Marble is primarily a coarse to fine-grained metamorphized limestone composed essentially of calcite and occasionally dolomite. The variety of colors found in marble are due to the many included impurities.

Marble forms in regions of metamorphism where molten igneous material came in contact with limestone or dolomite. If the original sediments were fairly pure, the resulting marble became coarsely crystalline and might exhibit nice white or colored hues. Marble is prized by lapidary craftsmen for its ability to take a polish.

□ MICA

Mica is actually a family of minerals. For our purposes, as beginners, they will all be grouped together. The most commonly encountered varieties of mica are muscovite and biotite.

Most Useful Clues For Identification: Mica is best identified by its thin flexible sheets which are easily separated. It is translucent to transparent and the sheet-like crystals are often found as hexagonal shaped bundles called "mica books."

Hardness: 2.5 - 3.0   **Specific Gravity:** 2.8
Streak: Colorless   **Fracture:** Uneven
Luster: Glassy or pearly   **Crystal System:** Monoclinic
Common Color(s): Muscovite: white, yellow, colorless, amber, rose, green.

Biotite: black, greenish black and brownish black.

Other Minerals Frequently Found With Mica: Quartz, orthoclase, microcline, albite, topaz, tourmaline, and beryl.

Where Found: Mica is often found in pegmatites and schists. It is also occasionally in association with igneous and metamorphic material. Rocks containing mica often glitter in the sunlight, making them somewhat easy to spot from a distance.

□ OBSIDIAN

A ROCK TYPE (Not a Mineral)

Obsidian is actually glass, the result of volcanic material being cooled so rapidly that it didn't have time to crystallize. Since it deteriorates quite rapidly (in geological terms), it is only found where volcanic activity has taken place in relatively recent times. Obsidian exhibits a conchoidal fracture and the edges of fracture surfaces can be quite sharp.

In order to find obsidian, look in regions of volcanic activity, near obvious volcanic flows. Quality varies greatly, and the transparent to translucent gem-grade varieties are not as often encountered as the more coarse material.

Obsidian tends to be gray or black, but sometimes it is streaked with other color, most frequently shades of chocolate brown. Due to internal planes resulting from the original molten flow, obsidian occasionally reflects light in a delicate iridescent green, violet, or silver hue. Such material is called rainbow obsidian. Small pebble-sized balls of volcanic glass are known as Apache tears and result from the weathering of larger obsidian deposits.

□ OPAL

Most Useful Clues For Identification: Opal is frequently confused with chalcedony, but it has a much more plastic-like fracture surface.

Hardness: 5.5 - 6.5	**Specific Gravity:** 2.0
Streak: White	**Fracture:** Conchoidal
Luster: Glassy or pearly	**Crystal System:** None

Common Color(s): Colorless or just about any other color, usually in light tints. Precious opal exhibits a sometimes spectacular rainbow play of colors.

Where Found: Opal is generally found in regions where there has been recent volcanic action, in deposits from hot springs, and in all types of silica rich sediments. It also replaces the skeletons of many microscopic plankton in the ocean. Opal is a fairly simple mineral that is created from water, silicon and oxygen. It is unusual because it is not composed of the ordered molecules that form symmetrical crystals. Because of its high water content, opal can be prone to cracking and dehydration. It ranges all the way from transparent to opaque.

Varieties of Opal:

Common Opal: Opal that does not show any internal play of colors.

Precious Opal: The variety of opal characterized by a sometimes spectacular internal play of colors.

Black Opal: These are a rare variety of precious opal that have a black, dark blue, or dark green body color combined with a play of color.

Fire Opal: A clear orange-red variety.

□ PYRITE

Most Useful Clues For Identification: Pyrite is easily identified by its tarnished gold color, metallic luster, hardness, and perfect cubic crystallization. It is opaque and the crystals are often striated. Pyrite is often referred to as "fools gold."

Hardness: 6.0 - 6.5　　　　**Specific Gravity:** 4.9 - 5.2
Streak: Brownish black　　　**Fracture:** Uneven
Luster: Metallic　　　　　**Crystal System:** Isometric
Common Color(s): Light brass-yellow

Other Minerals Frequently Found With Pyrite: Sphalerite, chalcopyrite, gold, and galena.

Where Found: Pyrite can be found in just about all types of rock and in most metal ore veins. The best specimens tend to come from hydrothermal regions, within slate and other metamorphic rocks, as well as pegmatites, limestone, and some schist shales.

□ QUARTZ

Most Useful Clues For Identification: Quartz exhibits a distinctive prismatic hexagonal crystallization, often with faces striated. It is quite hard, has a glasslike luster and a conchoidal fracture. It can vary from transparent to opaque, and includes just about every degree of transparency in between. It is the most common mineral in the earth's crust and, since it was one of the last to crystallize from molten lava, it frequently includes other minerals such as rutile, tourmaline, or actinolite.

Hardness: 7.0　　　　　　**Specific Gravity:** 2.65
Streak: White　　　　　　**Fracture:** Conchoidal (in crystalline
Luster: Glassy　　　　　　　　　　form), uneven to splintery (in
Crystal System: Hexagonal　　　　massive forms)
Common Color(s): Colorless, white, pink, smoky, rose, violet, brown, and many other subtle tints.

Where Found: Quartz can be found just about anywhere and crystals have been known to form in just about any type rock that has cavities. Pegmatites are famous for their spectacular quartz specimens, as are fissures in schists, sandstone, limestone, and certain contact zones. Voids in volcanic rock as well as the lining of hydrothermal veins often produce nice specimens. Inspect any type rock that seems porous and capable of possessing cavities.

Soft ash may have trapped gas bubbles which were subsequently filled with chalcedony or quartz, resulting in geodes or nodules (also see chalcedony). Mine dumps, placer workings, and gravel bars also offer a good opportunity for finding quartz.

Varieties of Quartz:

Amethyst: This is the best known transparent variety of quartz and it ranges in color from violet to red-purple.

Citrine: A transparent, yellow to orange-brown variety of quartz which sometimes resembles topaz.

Dumortierite: Dumortierite is a massive, opaque, deep blue or violet variety of quartz which looks very much like lapis-lazuli.

Milky Quartz: A massive white to light gray, translucent variety of quartz.

Rock Crystal: Purest form of quartz. It is optically colorless and transparent.

Rose Quartz: A usually massive, semitransparent to translucent type of quartz which occurs in various tones of pink.

Rutilated Quartz: A transparent variety of quartz characterized by the inclusions of golden, needle-like rutile.

Smoky Quartz: A transparent, smoky yellow to smoky brown variety of quartz.

□ SERPENTINE

Most Useful Clues For Identification: Serpentine is identified by its relative softness, compact massive appearance, green color, and waxy luster. It is generally translucent to opaque and is most valued as a carving material, sometimes used as a jade substitute.

Hardness: 3.0 - 5.0   **Specific Gravity:** 2.3 - 2.6
Streak: White (but may vary)   **Fracture:** Splintery or conchoidal
Luster: Silky or waxy   **Crystal System:** None (massive)
Common Color(s): White, green, brown, yellow, red, black.

Other Minerals Frequently Found With Serpentine: Magnesite, chromite, spinel, garnet and magnetite.

Where Found: Readily identifiable in highway cuts or in the field by the shiny, greenish, slick-sided surface of such exposures.

□ SILVER

Most Useful Clues For Identification: Silver is opaque and rarely encountered in crystallized form. Generally, it occurs as long, distorted wires, dendrites, or in a massive state. It is very malleable and ductile and is identified by its bright silver color (on untarnished surfaces), silvery white streak, and heavy weight.

Hardness: 2.5 - 3.0   **Specific Gravity:** 10.1 - 11.1
Streak: White (silvery)   **Fracture:** Hackly
Luster: Metallic   **Crystal System:** Isometric (rare)
Common Color(s): Fresh surface is bright white, but usually blackened by tarnish.

Other Minerals Frequently Found With Silver: Calcite, barite, quartz, fluorite, copper, nickel, and lead minerals.

Where Found: Usually found in ore veins.

□ TOURMALINE
Schoral, Dravite, Uvite, and Elbaite

Most Useful Clues For Identification: Tourmaline is identified by its long vertically striated crystals with rounded, bulging, triangular cross sections. It ranges from transparent to opaque and some of the crystals can be very large and/or colorful. In the colored crystals, the hue frequently changes from one end to the other or from center to surface.

Hardness: 7.0 - 7.5   **Specific Gravity:** 3.0 - 3.3
Streak: White   **Fracture:** Uneven or conchoidal
Luster: Glassy   **Crystal System:** Hexagonal
Common Color(s): Black (schoral), brown or garnet-red (dravite), pink (rubellite), white (uvite), green (verdelite), blue (indicolite), and multi-hued (elbaite).

Other Minerals Frequently Found With Tourmaline: Quartz, andalusite, muscovite, lepidolite, feldspar, topaz, zircon, beryl, apatite, spodumene, and microcline.

Where Found: Tourmaline is most frequently found in granite pegmatites, but it also occurs in some schists and, occasionally, in hydrothermal deposits.

CHAPTER 6 FINDING MINERALS IN THE FIELD

Now that you have been inundated with information, it is time to head for the field and actually find some minerals. Be sure that your first trips are restricted to known productive sites, as provided in guidebooks or recent magazine articles, in order to assure that something worthwhile can be found. Before discussing specific things to look for when in the field, however, it is essential that we first go over a few rules of courtesy and safety.

☞ First and foremost, be certain not to trespass onto someone's property. A guidebook or magazine article is usually accurate in providing ownership status at the time of publication, but that may have changed.

☞ Be well informed about all laws and regulations governing any region within which you intend to collect. If you are unsure, make local inquiry. Some areas afford unrestricted collecting while there may be limits or restrictions at others.

☞ When you arrive at a collecting area, take a few moments to survey the region, carefully looking for potential hazards. These include nails, glass, chemicals, diggings and/or open pits, steep cliffs, poisonous or irritating shrubs, potential for snakes, etc.

☞ If you find that a portion of a collecting site is fenced off, do not disregard the barrier, since it is probably there for a purpose!

☞ Caves and abandoned mines present obvious hazards, as do flooded gravel pits and quarries. Do not enter any such areas.

PHOTO 24 *No matter how inviting, never enter an abandoned mine shaft.*

☞ Never work above or below a person on a steep cliff, since rock may be dislodged resulting in injury. Use common sense. Do not put yourself in any situation which could be dangerous either to you or to someone else.

☞ Beach areas need to be treated with respect or you might find yourself trapped by an incoming tide. Know when high and low tides occur and plan accordingly.

☞ If you are going to remote areas, be sure to let someone know where you will be. It is also advisable not to go alone. Two vehicles offer insurance in the event one becomes stuck or breaks down.

☞ Don't use firearms or blasting material. Not only is that dangerous, but it will most likely damage the minerals you are seeking.

PHOTO 25 *If you choose to do some digging, be sure to refill all excavations. Not only are the holes unsightly, but they might also be hazardous to cattle or other wildlife.*

☞ It might be tempting to break up what appears to be an old building or sign for use in a campfire. PLEASE do not do that. What might appear as derelict may not actually be, and if signs and/or buildings are damaged by thoughtless collectors, sites might be closed to all. Respect the rights of others.

☞ If you choose to build a campfire, do so in a safe spot and be certain it is completely extinguished before leaving the area

☞ Do not leave trash and, by all means, do not contaminate any water supply, including wells, streams, ponds, or lakes.

☞ Take along some extra supplies such as tools for auto repair, food, and water in the event you get stuck or delayed.

☐ FINALLY, INTO THE FIELD!

Now let us get on with the task of finding something. How do you spot situations conducive to mineral production such as pegmatites, contact zones, or any of the other geological conditions discussed in Chapter 1? Always keep in mind, as has been mentioned so many times earlier, the single most important factor related to successful collecting is EXPERIENCE! After visiting numerous sites over the years, there will be certain characteristics of the landscape or other subtle clues that will intuitively guide you to the best spots. Until you gain that experience, however, the following information should prove to be useful. We will first look at the most prolific mineralogical environments and then present some additional tips.

Pegmatites

As you remember from Chapter 1, pegmatites originate in cracks formed when molten igneous masses were cooling. The still liquid rock trapped deep within the outer hardening mass sometimes squeezed into those cracks due to the immense internal pressure, resulting in a pegmatite. Pegmatites sometimes provide the space and chemical isolation necessary for the formation of more pure minerals and are renown for their sometimes spectacular crystal content. Minerals often associated with pegmatites include mica, feldspar, beryl, quartz, and tourmaline.

Not all pegmatites are mineralogically productive, however, since the opportunity to provide a situation conducive to crystal growth not only depends upon what is present in the original molten lava, but also the existence of enough space within the cracks and fractures to provide growing room.

To identify an exposed pegmatite in the field look for differences in the terrain. Pegmatites tend to decompose much more rapidly than the harder encasing granite or other native rock. That conspicuous decomposition often forms rounded hills and soil which can support plant life.

PHOTO 26 *A granite outcrop with vegetation indicating the potential for a pegmatite or other regions of mineralization. Naushon Island, Massachusetts.*

Look for rounded, weathered rock in brush covered areas and forget about places with barren granite (Photo 27). Search for definite differences in weathering patterns, with the pegmatite regions being more decomposed than other rock (Photo 28). Pegmatites sometimes appear whitish in color, so look for light colored nodules and ribs against the darker soil of the mountainsides.

PHOTO 27

Examining a pegmatite deposit in southwest Colorado.

PHOTO 28 *A pegmatite (white) running through a deposit of gneiss. In Jefferson County, Colorado.*

Since quartz is very hard and resistant to decomposition, as well as being a major component of most mineralogically significant pegmatites, it is usually a reliable indicator. If you come upon blocks of quartz scattered about, usually white and sometimes containing feldspar, you may be near a pegmatite. If some of the quartz exhibits regions of transparency, especially if smoky, or if there are occasional embedded crystals of tourmaline, you may be on to something with great potential.

Contact Zones

Contact zones are usually quite easy to spot in the field. Remember that they are the result of molten magma coming in contact with solid existing rock. Simply look for two distinctly different types of rock butted up against each other or one penetrating the other. The area in and around the surfaces where the magma encountered the original rock is the contact zone. It can often be a source of minerals, either the result of metamorphic crystallization or secondary crystal growth in voids within the region of contact. (Photo 29 and also refer to Photos 13 & 14 from Chapter 1).

Two of the most common contact zone scenarios are (1) when lava flows over the existing rock, and (2) when extreme subsurface pressures force molten material into existing rock. The latter intrusion, referred to as a dike, usually enters the native rock in regions of weakness, such as preexisting cracks or layers. This is very similar to pegmatite creation, except that pegmatites formed as the entire mass was solidifying, while contact zones were created by rock from distinctly different geological time periods. A few desirable contact minerals include hematite, corundum, pyrite, graphite, garnet, galena, spinel, tourmaline, topaz, and fluorite.

PHOTO 29 *A classic contact zone. Once molten lava (dark) on top of limestone (white). Near Barstow, California.*

Metamorphic Situations

As we discussed in Chapter 1, metamorphic rocks are the consequence of immense heat and pressure placed on existing igneous, sedimentary or other metamorphic rocks. When those forces are sufficiently intense, the original stone is altered into something completely different.

Metamorphic rock is usually quite easy to distinguish when in the field. It is often contorted, frequently exhibits streaking, in contrasting colors, and possesses the ability to split away in sheets (Photo 30 and also refer to Photo 7 from Chapter 1).

PHOTO 30 *A small pegmatite running vertically through a metamorphic schist deposit.*

Which minerals can be found within metamorphic rock depends upon what it started as and what mineralization was added during the process of metamorphism. Outstanding specimens of garnet, mica, kyanite, and corundum are known to come from metamorphic rock.

Schist is generally one of the most productive metamorphic rock types. Schist outcrops are usually easy to spot, since they are somewhat dark, ragged, and show contorted layering. Many schists contain good quantities of mica and thereby glisten in the sunlight. There are many types of schists, but if you happen upon a good one, keep your eyes out for garnet crystals, mica, feldspar, corundum, and jadeite.

Marble, yet another metamorphic rock, is not only desirable in its own right, but also might contain quartz and calcite crystals, as well as sometimes beautiful specimens of mica, corundum, garnet, serpentine, brown tourmaline, and spinel.

Exposed marble deposits are somewhat easy to spot, while in the field, appearing as bright white rounded little hills and knobs, often associated with vegetation. The surface, upon closer examination, is often severely etched, due to its susceptibility to weathering. In addition, most marble has a very uniform texture; it is easily scratched by a knife, and a freshly exposed surface will sparkle in the sunlight.

Serpentine is yet another metamorphic rock also desirable in its own right. It is often used as a jade substitute and is relatively easy to spot, due to its green color. Outcrops are usually quite rounded and might even be covered by scant vegetation (Photo 31). Look for the light green or greenish gray greasy color, with somewhat rough edged fractures. Serpentine deposits occasionally offer collectors specimens of chalcedony, asbestos, jade (both jadeite and nephrite), and rhodonite.

PHOTO 31 *Parked next to a huge serpentine deposit in Northern California that was exposed by a roadcut.*

Sedimentary Mineral Occurrences

Sedimentary rock results from massive accumulations of small rock and mineral grains, as well as any other debris that may have become captured in the process. It is usually easy to spot while in the field, due to the obvious layering which results from different periods of sedimentation. In addition, sedimentary rock is somewhat grainy and easily broken up (Photo 32).

PHOTO 32 *A nice and easily spotted example of layered shale. Near Salina, Utah.*

Mounds of clay, ash or mud should more properly be referred to as sedimentary deposits rather than sedimentary rock, since they have not been compressed into stone. These badlands-like formations result from heavily eroded ancient lake or sea beds and are usually easy to spot in the field (Photos 33 & 34). Some are treasure troves for fossils, petrified wood, selenite and a number of other more obscure minerals.

Limestone is another sedimentary rock of interest to mineral collectors, usually quite easy to spot in the field due to its whitish gray color and pocked surface. It often contains cavities filled with sometimes beautiful crystallized barite, calcite, chalcedony, gypsum, fluorite, and selenite, as well as galena and

PHOTO 33 *Unusual mounds near Fallon, Nevada that yielded good collecting.*

pyrite cubes. Onyx is the fine grained and often eloquently banded variety of limestone highly regarded for lapidary use.

69

PHOTO 34 *Searching for petrified wood and selenite in the remnants of an ancient sea near Coaldale, Nevada.*

□ MORE TIPS TO ASSURE SUCCESSFUL COLLECTING

☞ Probably the one most important suggestion for increasing your chances of finding worthwhile mineral specimens is to look for something unusual. That might be a weirdly contorted rock, or vividly contrasting rock types or colors, a glisten in the sunlight, or any variety of sometimes subtle things that catch your eye. (Photo 35).

PHOTO 35 *Look for something unusual such as this porous granite cut by dikes, veins, and filled fractures. Near Acton, California.*

☞ Be sure to keep an eye out for other minerals which might be associated with those desired. If you find something known to occur in conjunction with what you are looking for, that can be of great help in narrowing down where you might spend some time. Some of these associations are presented in Chapter 5.

☞ Know what types of geological situations are conducive to the formation of mineral(s) you are searching for. Geodes and thunder eggs are found in volcanic areas; tourmaline, feldspar, quartz, beryl and kunzite within pegmatites; heavy minerals such as garnet and corundum can be found settling in the lower parts of gravel beds; etc.

☞ Start at a known mineral-producing location, but always keep in mind that just because a guidebook says to go a specific number of miles to a collecting site, does not mean you will then be in its center or even at the most productive area. Be willing to do some hiking and exploration to find the best specimens.

☞ Taking a hike downslope or downstream from productive deposits or old mines can very often be fruitful (Photo 36). Some fine gemstones have been found in this manner. It is only natural that most people tend to concentrate their enthusiasm on the primary source and do not even consider what may have been transported away by the forces of nature.

PHOTO 36 *Exploring the region downstream from a mine dump in the Calico Mountains of California.*

☞ If you find a good mineral deposit, always keep in mind that similar nearby geologic situations might afford additional or even better specimens. Pay particularly close attention to the surroundings in known sites which are productive and then do some hiking or driving, keeping an eye out for similar settings. If you find good specimens on one side of a mountain or valley, try the other side, or the next hill, or canyon, or wash, etc.

☞ Pay attention to regions which are relatively clear of vegetation. It is much easier to see suspicious geological formations on barren rock. Once you spot something interesting, you can expand the search to adjacent areas which may be partially obscured by trees and shrubs.

☞ Stones in washes, ravines and stream beds often provide a good sampling of what can be found nearby and/or upstream. If you spot something of interest, try to determine from where it might have come. Search the surrounding countryside as you trek upstream for some of the landmarks discussed earlier. If you reach a point where you no longer can find anything of interest in the wash or stream, double back, since you have probably passed the source. (Photo 37).

☞ In places that were once known to be rich producers of minerals, the surface may have been picked over. In those cases, be especially attentive for even a small corner or edge of rock sticking up from the ground and then dig it out. Additional digging at that spot may lead to even more.

PHOTO 37 *Exploring a wash near Cave Creek, Arizona to get a good idea of what can be found upstream.*

☞ Don't neglect the flatlands below suspect and sometimes inaccessible geological formations. Generally, any minerals that were deposited on a flatland were probably transported there by floods or other forces of erosion (Photo 38). Chances are that the minerals have been scattered in varying concentrations for quite a distance, requiring a willingness to do some walking. A good technique to use when searching flatlands is to hike in a crisscross fashion with the sun at many angles to the direction you are proceeding. Some minerals, such as agate, jasper, and chalcedony tend to be easier to spot if the sun is directly ahead or to the side, while others, such as Apache tears or extremely colorful minerals, tend to be best seen with the sun to your back.

☞ If you stumble upon quartz crystals possessing good, sharp faces, they might indicate a nearby productive cavity or seam and efforts should be intensified to locate where they came from. In addition, if you spot mica books, tourmaline and/or feldspar crystals, you may be near a gem-bearing pegmatite.

PHOTO 38 *Searching the flatlands below igneous mountains in Arizona.*

☞ Carefully inspect porous boulders and rock, even if encountered in a wash or plain, since they might contain pockets of crystals or other minerals.

☞ When you encounter a promising but heavily weathered rock that doesn't look too promising on the surface, be sure to split it with a rock pick to ascertain its true desirability. Weathered surfaces sometimes tend to be misleading and obscure a stone's true nature.

PHOTO 39 *Inspecting an old pegmatite mine dump (don't enter the shaft) in New Hampshire.*

☞ Quarries and mine dumps (Photos 39 & 40) not only offer great potential for finding minerals but also provide an opportunity to observe the geological setting associated with those minerals. As mentioned previously, be observant of geological formations associated with mineral production in order to enhance subsequent field trips.

PHOTO 40 *Some suspicious diggings in Colorado.*

☞ When exploring a mine or quarry, keep an eye out for anything that looks a little different. It might be an unusual color, texture, porosity, shape, or any other "out of the ordinary" characteristic.

☞ In volcanic areas, the rock is sometimes porous enough for circulating water to deposit chalcedony, crystalline quartz, or other minerals. Look for very contorted or porous spots, since they are the most likely to possess these mineral-filled openings and voids (Photo 41).

PHOTO 41 *Look for volcanic areas since these are the most conducive to having openings and voids which may contain crystals. This deposit is north of Milford, Utah.*

☞ Search for outcrops and other rock which appears to be deteriorating, "rotting," or porous, since such situations are often associated with mineralization (Photo 42).

☞ Since granite is usually quite uniform in texture and grain, anything out of the ordinary should be of interest. The more easily a granite decomposes and crumbles, the more likely it is to possess good mineral specimens. In such situations look for black tourmaline, garnet, feldspar, fluorite, quartz, topaz, beryl, and zircon.

PHOTO 42 *A suspiciously rotting outcrop in southwest Colorado.*

☞ Many nice specimens can be found in hydrothermal veins, formed when dissolved minerals were forced into openings by superheated water (see Chapter 1). Look for areas where there may have been weakness, whether it be a crack, or fault, or contact zone. Within those areas might be voids conducive to crystallization or deposition of minerals. A good clue is the presence of trees or shrubs growing on what appears to be a sheer rock wall. That often indicates a mineralized cavity or crack within which it has sent its roots. (Photos 42 & 43 and also refer to Photos 11 & 12 from Chapter 1).

☞ Look for brightly colored "stains" on the native rock. The copper ores of chrysocolla, malachite and azurite are bright blues and greens, while iron ores generally tend to be red, brown and orange. Manganese oxides are usually black, cobalt is lilac, while lead and molybdenum are customarily light yellow. These stains are usually easy to spot and could indicate the presence of something worthwhile.

PHOTO 43 *A vertical fault line from the Gallatin Valley of California.*

☞ Look around the borders of large masses of granite, both in the granite itself and the surrounding rock. Such areas are sometimes known to produce interesting minerals.

PHOTO 44 *A crack created by a small fault in the Catalina Mountains of Arizona.*

☞ In just about any type of native rock, if it is cut by a dike or any other igneous intrusion, especially if light in color, there is possibility for mineralization, particularly at the spot where the native rock and the intrusion meet (refer to Photos 28, 30, & 35 and Photos 9, 10 & 14 from Chapter 1).

In fact, any exposed rock consisting of obviously dissimilar constituents representing different times of formation can be mineralogically productive. Be particularly attentive for distinct changes in coloration or a layered appearance. (Photos 30 & 45 and also refer to Photos 12, 13 & 14 from Chapter 1).

☞ If you spot a substantial quartz vein or dike, examine it carefully for crystals, since it might contain pockets. Gem and crystal pockets in such formations are usually more toward the central and thickest portion.

☞ If at all possible, a good time to conduct your search is shortly after a rainstorm, since the water cleanses the surface and intensifies the colors and texture. If collecting after a rain is impractical, take a little spray bottle filled with water to clean a specimen and enhance the colors in order to determine desirability. Severely abraded stones may have to first be split in order to provide a more reliable surface.

PHOTO 45 *Joints in granite cut by dissimilar veins of quartz, feldspar, and biotite mica. Las Animas Canyon, Colorado.*

☞ Ancient sea and lake beds can furnish collectors with fine mineral specimens. The lake beds are usually easy to distinguish, being either sandy and/or flat, sometimes slightly depressed, and whitish in color, especially in desert regions. Minerals can be readily spotted against the fairly uniform and flat soil and the list of what can be found includes selenite, petrified wood, fossils, agate, jasper, or just about anything else, depending upon what occurs in the surrounding terrain.

PHOTO 46 *Searching along the freshly exposed shores of a receding lake in central Nevada.*

☞ During the summer months, it is sometimes worthwhile to search along rivers, creeks, lakes, and reservoirs (Photo 46). At that time of year, unless it has been an especially wet winter, those bodies of water may be very low or even completely dry, exposing otherwise submerged regions. Be careful not to wade into an unsafe area, however. In addition, do not waste your time in regions not known for minerals.

☞ If in a highly vegetated region, observe the various types of brush and other foliage. There is usually a distinct dissimilarity of what grows in different types of soil and this dissimilarity can often be spotted from quite a distance. The region in and around such abrupt changes in soil and/or rock may be good areas to explore.

☞ Road cuts (Photos 31 & 47) and even construction sites are famous for exposing great mineral deposits. Look wherever fresh rock is exposed.

☞ Always try to make a record, both written and photographic, if possible, related to any worthwhile find. Note, specifically, the location and anything particularly unusual about the surrounding terrain. Such notes and photos will help you to locate other similar settings.

PHOTO 47 *Inspecting a portion of a pegmatite exposed in a roadcut in south-central Utah.*

☞ Alluvial deposits are concentrations of specific heavy and durable minerals (Photo 48). Some of the more commonly encountered alluvial or placer minerals are gold, diamond, garnet, corundum, zircon, and topaz. A more detailed look at alluvial minerals is presented in Chapter 8.

PHOTO 48 *Searching for heavy minerals (primarily gold) in an alluvial deposit near Fairbanks, Alaska.*

7 SPECIAL COLLECTING TECHNIQUES

Gathering minerals in a secondary deposit is usually fairly simple. For the most part it involves bending over and picking up the specimens or, possibly, if at an unusually challenging site, using a pick and shovel to get buried material. Working primary deposits, however, usually necessitates much more. You will need determination, ingenuity, patience, and a willingness to do some hard work. For that reason, this chapter is primarily devoted toward the extraction of minerals from primary sources. It is hoped that these suggestions will help you recover nice minerals with minimal damage.

PHOTO 49 *Attacking a primary deposit for Herkimer Diamonds in New York.*

In order to work a primary deposit you must have the appropriate tools, and they can be quite heavy and cumbersome. Do not be tempted to use ordinary workshop tools, since they are not designed for the immense forces associated with breaking down solid rock. It is essential that you use equipment specifically designed for such application and a complete discussion of options is provided in Chapter 3.

□ GENERAL TECHNIQUES FOR SPLITTING SEAMS OR ENTERING CAVITIES

How you approach opening a seam or widening a cavity largely depends upon the nature of exactly what is being collected and the composition of the surrounding rock. Some cavities or cracks might be filled with fragile crystals, while, in other situations, the mineral of interest may be solid veins of chalcedony or agate. Different types of minerals and occurrences may require significantly different collecting approaches.

PHOTO 50 *Looking for signs of weakness in a pegmatite deposit (notice the many possibilities in the cracks and seams).*

The first step is to carefully examine the rock surrounding the cavity or seam you are trying to access. An unfractured, fine-grained igneous rock is much more difficult to break down then a highly weathered, porous or fractured counterpart. Pounding on solid rock surrounding a cavity or seam will generally do nothing more than create a little white dust at the spot you make contact. You have to formulate a strategy. In the case of hard rock work, that strategy may very well necessitate removing a much larger portion of the surrounding material than you may initially think necessary.

PHOTO 51 *Breaking up fossil-bearing shale along natural fracture and bedding lines near Danby, California.*

PHOTO 52

Examining a shale deposit in Utah to find which of the numerous bedding and fracture areas can be used to procure the largest specimens.

First, look for some nearby indication of weakness. (Photos 50, 51 & 52) That might be a crack, natural fault, fissure, contact zone, a region of porosity or decay, or any other sign of unsoundness. When you locate such a spot, if it exists, try to use a gad, heavy pry bar, and/or any other type wedge to widen it in an attempt to break off a portion of the encasing host rock. If you have many choices of fractures or cracks to work with, it might be helpful to use more than one at a time. Progress slowly and don't be afraid to try different approaches in order to eventually allow removal of the largest portion of the seam or cavity as possible (Photo 53). As you work, pay close attention to what is happening. If you are crushing the crystals or fracturing the included minerals, stop and reconsider the plan of attack. It makes absolutely no sense to work so hard just to destroy everything.

A technique which can be used to help protect crystals in a cavity or seam while it is being broken down involves stuffing rags or paper into the void.

PHOTO 53 *Sometimes it's better to use a pry bar and its associated leverage to break off portions of rotten rock.*

This will not only help prevent crystals from breaking loose or being otherwise damaged, but it also helps absorb shock from the pounding, thereby lessening the likelihood of fracture.

If you are working on a lengthy crack, try pounding gads and wedges into a number of different locations along its length to see the effect. Some places might be better, in respect to leverage and weakness of the rock, than others.

Always try to remove sections much larger than you think you want. No matter how careful you work, whatever is eventually removed will end up being significantly smaller than planned. If you happen to be lucky and in fact do remove something surprisingly large, think of all the possibilities. It can be carefully separated into more than one specimen or the more sizable chunk might turn out to be a real prize, as is. In addition, the larger piece will allow for more flexibility in trimming. Usually regions around the edge will incur some damage during the removal process. If your specimen is large enough, those areas can be trimmed away, leaving a far more showy piece.

□ WORKING A PEGMATITE

If you discover a potentially productive pegmatite, there are a number of ways to proceed. The techniques discussed in the proceeding paragraphs offer some good suggestions. It should be kept in mind that cavities contained in pegmatites are often filled with clay or other mineralogical debris and the crystals are oftentimes loose and embedded within that material.

Follow the guidelines outlined above to provide an access to the cavity which is wide enough for your hand or some sort of small scraping tool to reach inside. Your hand would be the better choice, since it will not damage the often fragile crystals and, furthermore, the sense of feel is very helpful in determining the layout of the cavity. If the clay is hard, however, you may need a screwdriver or some sort of probe to break it down, but, as mentioned earlier, be very careful, since some pegmatite crystals, especially when first being exposed to the air, can be quite delicate and easily damaged.

Remove as much of the cavity material as possible and place it in a bucket of water so the clay can be broken down and the crystals cleaned. If some crystals remain attached to the cavity walls, proceed as described earlier.

□ REMOVING ROCK PROTUBERANCES, KNOBS, ETC.

If you are removing a mineral-bearing projection, concentrate your efforts at the base, near where it emanates from the host rock . If not too large, a few well placed blows with a sturdy sledge hammer should break it free. Be very careful, however, that you do not damage whatever you are trying to get. Once the protuberance starts to crack, try inserting a gad or other similar tool into that crack to finish the job with more control and less shock (Photo 54). Once completely dislodged from its place on the mountain, the minerals being sought can be more carefully recovered, trimmed and sized.

PHOTO 54 *Using (left to right) a large gad, pry bar and a smaller gad to break off a piece of rock from its place on the hillside.*

□ WORKING ON MINE DUMPS

The first two rules for collecting at mine dumps are (1) be sure it is safe, and (2) be certain collecting is allowed there. What might at first appear to be an abandoned prospect may still be privately owned. Claimholders are usually not very receptive to the idea of someone taking minerals from their mine, at least without first getting permission to do so. If you are not sure about land status, find out by either contacting the appropriate county recorder's office or making some sort of local inquiry.

It is also necessary to again remind you to never enter a shaft, no matter how promising it might appear. Restrict your collecting to the dumps. This makes good sense, not only from a safety point of view, but also from a mineral collector's point of view. Most abandoned mines were not originally constructed to recover crystals and secondary minerals, and such material was regarded as uninteresting waste and simply discarded. Try to determine what type of associated minerals and the extent of crystallization was originally present at the mine you plan to inspect. If no crystallization was present, which is rare, then digging might be a waste of time and effort, but, if there were some interesting secondary minerals, they are probably still somewhere in the dump.

A very important fact to keep in mind when working at old mines is that the best specimens generally tend to be found within the oldest portions of any given dump. This is primarily due to the fact that until somewhat recent times prospectors were only able to extract the mineral(s) they were mining from regions of greatest concentration. More recent mining activities, however, may have employed new technologies capable of extracting even minute traces of gold, silver, copper or whatever else the miners were looking for from just about all rock. That means that virtually nothing of collectable interest was left behind, since it was probably crushed and processed with everything else.

You obviously can't dig directly down to the bottom of a dump to those older regions, but sometimes such areas can be accessed by going in from the side at a lower or intermediate spot. Don't waste much time on the front slopes of any dump since that is where the most recent rock has been discarded. Go to the sides or inspect heavily eroded places where older material might be more accessible.

Another technique which might prove fruitful when exploring an abandoned mining area is to search in regions covered by shrubs or trees. Obviously, this makes the effort more challenging, but that is the very reason such places might provide better specimens. Prior rockhounds may have avoided such spots due to the effort required. You might, therefore, be the first to actually examine rock from those spots since it originally came to rest there.

Try to locate other less accessible, hidden or obscured regions, and also be sure to carefully inspect territory below and downstream, since potentially valuable material may have been washed there many years ago, where it has remained ever since.

Break up suspicious boulders or sizable chunks of rock, since they might contain cavities or otherwise concealed regions of desirability. When you find something worthwhile on a dump, carefully note the level, location, color, texture and other distinguishing characteristics of the associated rock. Then look elsewhere for the same combinations.

□ A FEW MORE SUGGESTIONS

☞ When working a contact zone, use the same hints as provided with seams and cracks in the earlier part of this chapter.

☞ If you encounter a large boulder or rock in a known mineral rich area, try to break it down with a sledge hammer, gads, pry bars, and/or chisels to better ascertain exactly what it has to offer. Freshly exposed surfaces will give a much better indication of its desirability. If there is something worthwhile, it can be further broken down.

☞ If you find surface specimens which tend to be quite weathered and decomposed, you might consider doing some digging in hopes of finding material that has not been as exposed to the weather.

☞ Decomposed rock is normally somewhat crumbly and easy to break up. As you carefully work into such material, it is important to meticulously examine all that is being removed. There could be "rotted" traces of crystals or minerals indicating the presence of something potentially worthwhile further in. Do not be discouraged if these "indicators" look worn and worthless because of weathering.

☞ Screening provides an excellent method for finding gemstones in gravel, especially if water is accessible. Simply construct a wooden frame with a heavy

PHOTO 55 *Searching for gemstones using a screening box near Helena, Wyoming.*

duty, fine mesh screen nailed to the bottom (Photos 55 & 56). Place gem- or mineral-bearing gravel onto the screen and either rinse from above or dip the entire frame, gravel and all, into and out of a body of water such as a stream or lake. After all of the dirt and small rock fragments have washed through the screen, carefully sort through what remains for signs of color, transparency, etc. This is an excellent way to probe secondary deposits for tough gemstones such as sapphires, rubies and garnets. In addition, outstanding agates, jaspers, and other hard minerals can also be found in this manner.

☞ If working in soft sedimentary type materials such as clays, shales and some sandstones, breaking it down usually takes a minimal effort. Use a hand rake or trowel or, in some cases, even your hands, to dig into the somewhat soft encasing material in search of minerals and/or fossils.

PHOTO 56 *Using wooden framed screens to sort out gem-bearing gravel near Fernwood, Idaho.*

□ COLLECTING FOSSILS

Even though this book primarily deals with rocks, minerals and gemstones, if you spend much time in the field, you will surely encounter some fossils. In fact, many rockhounds also become avid fossil collectors. Below are listed a few tips specifically related to gathering fossils, but, keep in mind that many of the techniques discussed for extracting minerals also apply. Fossils, however, tend to be easily decomposed, thereby limiting the number of quality examples that can be found in secondary deposits. The abrasion and tumbling generated by the forces of nature will frequently destroy all but the most solid. Petrified material, however, is quite different. That consists of fossils whose cells and internal structure have been entirely replaced by silica (chalcedony). In fact, they are actually stones and can be treated as such!

☞ If you are looking for fossils, it is suggested that you take, in addition to the earlier mentioned equipment, a screwdriver, knife, paintbrush, white glue, extra water, little boxes, and some clear spray acrylic.

☞ Just as was the case with minerals, there are many excellent fossil collecting guidebooks on the market, and it would be well worth the small expense to obtain one that covers the area you plan to visit.

☞ Fossils are most frequently found in sedimentary rock, so carefully inspect any suspect limestone, sandstone, shale, or peat bog, especially if exposed in road cuts, railroad cuts, or other such excavation sites. Search regions below promising sedimentary formations for traces of fossils in an effort to better pinpoint where the best can be found.

☞ If you are looking in shale or bedded limestone, start peeling off each layer with the aid of a knife or small chisel, one layer at a time, and carefully check each subsequent surface for indications of ancient life forms. Work slowly and carefully, though, since fossils tend to be somewhat fragile. It is a good idea, as was the case when trying to remove portions of crystal seams and cavities, to procure as large a portion of the encasing and surrounding rock as possible. Then, once removed, you can take it to a more convenient location for more careful separation, trimming, and inspection.

☞ If the fossil or encasing material tends to be unstable or crumbly, it is a good idea to give it a fine spray with clear acrylic paint. That will help hold things together until you can get it home for better evaluation and reinforcement. Another means of stabilizing fragile fossils is to brush them with white, water soluble glue which has been diluted with water.

☞ If you find a particularly productive fossil layer in a sedimentary formation, it might prove fruitful to attempt exploring other portions of that bedding plane, since the entire length was laid down during the same geological time and under the same circumstances. By doing that, you may find a spot that is considerably more accessible, productive, and/or easy to work.

CHAPTER 8 GOLD & OTHER SIMILAR MINERALS

This chapter deals with finding heavy and resilient minerals such as gold, corundum, garnet, and diamonds. There is also a short discussion related to the applicability of using a metal detector in certain special situations.

□ PLACER DEPOSITS

A placer deposit refers to concentrations of minerals placed somewhere away from where they were originally formed. There are four types of interest to the beginning rockhound and, before we get into a detailed discussion of how to recover minerals from such a deposit, it is important to first understand what they are and how they form.

Residual Placer

A residual placer (Diagram 1) is a mineral concentration caused by the host rock decaying. The rain, wind and other forces of nature break down rock, freeing the included minerals. As the debris near the deposit further disintegrates, crystals and minerals that are more immune to weathering will remain. Such an accumulation of rotting rocks, at or near the original deposit, is termed a residual placer.

Eluvial Placer

The second type of placer (Diagram 1) represents yet the next step in the natural erosion and weathering process. When minerals are freed from their place in the surrounding rock, the actions of water, earthquakes, wind, gravity, etc. cause them to gradually be carried away. These deposits are called eluvial placers. The harder, less easily fractured crystals and gemstones will tend to be quite rough and often still partially attached to fragments of the original host rock.

Stream Placers

Also known as alluvial desposits, (Diagram 1) these type of placers are next in the sequence. Forces of nature scatter the more hardy minerals, as described above, and this "traveling" often brings them to a stream or river. Once there, the often violent action of the water starts its ruthless beating and churning, causing the still attached host rock to gradually be reduced and eventually removed from the more durable gemstones and minerals. As these minerals travel down the stream, the heaviest of them, including gold, garnet, pyrite, silver, corundum, topaz, hematite and galena will sink and settle into the gravel, at often predictable locations which will be discussed later.

The term *bench placer* (Diagram 1) or terrace deposit is used to describe a special type of stream placer. The difference is that there is no longer water in the stream, usually due to a geological uplift. These ancient beds can be as much as fifty to many hundreds of feet higher than present streams in the same locality but still can posses great quantities of gold and other heavy minerals.

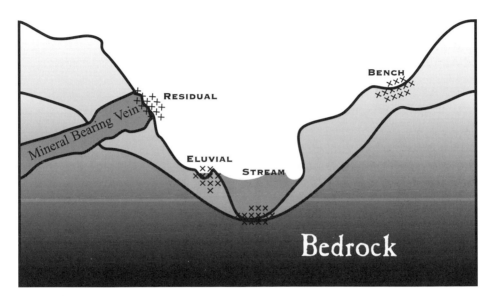

DIAGRAM 1 *Some typical types of placers.*

Bajada Placers

Bajada placers (Diagram 2) are those found in arid regions, near the bases of mineral-bearing mountains. The initial geologic stages are the same as those for the stream deposits, but, in these locations there are few streams flowing except during torrential rainstorms and floods. At the point where a mountain's base comes in contact with the smaller foothills, there is a substantial decrease in steepness. These lower slopes are referred to as bajadas and heavy minerals can sometimes be found concentrated there.

When the water rushes down the main mountain and reaches the bajada, its velocity is decreased because of the considerably lessened angle of descent. If the water contains heavy and durable minerals, it will lose them there, because their weight will cause them to settle, and only the lighter materials will continue to be carried farther in the now slower moving water. The area nearest the base of the major mountain thrust is where the majority of these minerals will be, if there are any to be found. Through the years, with countless floods, the thusly deposited minerals will eventually sink until reaching bedrock.

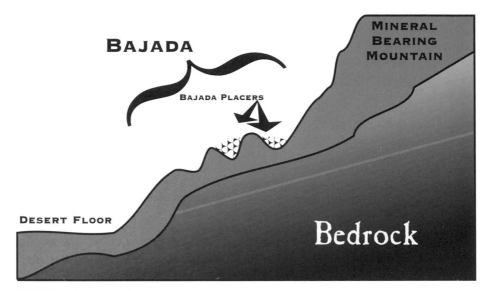

A bajada placer.

▫ THE GEOLOGY OF A STREAM

Probably the most reliable source of concentrated heavy minerals are the stream placers. This is because the forces associated with the running water serves as an ongoing, continual concentration process. If you want to attempt finding concentrations of heavy and durable minerals such as garnet, corundum, diamonds, gold, silver, pyrite, quartz, topaz or hematite in streams, it might be helpful to further examine specific factors that tend to enhance your chances. Listed below are some of those situations which cause heavy minerals to concentrate in waterways:

(1) As gold and the other heavy gemstones and minerals are transported downstream, they, along with larger boulders and other heavy materials, will take the shortest route, this being from inside bend to inside bend, hugging the curve as they go (Diagram 3-A). The greater the bend, the slower the velocity on the inside. The reduction of speed often causes them to settle and burrow into the mud, making such places good areas to look. The heavier minerals, including gold, will generally be more concentrated on the upstream portion of the curve, due to the current's rapid deceleration at that point. If the curve is more gradual, however, they could theoretically be deposited just about anywhere along it.

(2) Directly related to (1), above, gemstones and heavy minerals will sink

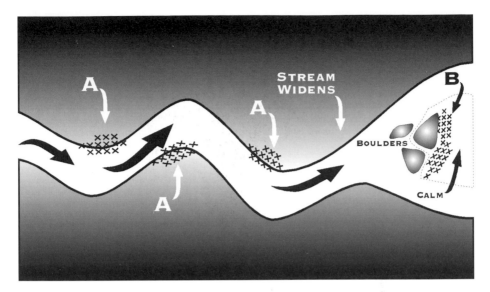

DIAGRAM 3 *Gold often settles on the inside and upstream edge of a sharp bend in a waterway (A) or at a point where it substantially widens, especially if there is some sort of obstruction at that point (B).*

when the current slows, no matter what the cause. Look along the river for places where gravel and boulders have been accumulating. This is an indication that something, whether visible or submerged, is slowing or blocking the water.

(3) Look for any type of obstruction in the river. Fallen trees, large boulders (Diagram 4-D) and groups of boulders are just a few examples. Generally speaking, the gold, gemstones and other heavy minerals will collect on the downstream side of these impediments due to the inherent eddies. An eddy is simply a backward and downward swirling current which is caused by the obstacle that sucks the minerals behind it. Sometimes, however, the stones do become trapped on the upstream side, so it wouldn't hurt to look there also.

(4) If the stream widens within a very short distance (Diagram 3-B), the result will be a rapid slowing of the current, and such an area is often productive. Any boulders or other obstacles, as mentioned above, will be even more effective in catching the now sinking gems, gold and heavy minerals.

(5) If there is a bedrock projection from a side into the stream, or an extremely sharp turn, these too, can concentrate heavy minerals. There are three variations of interest to beginners:

☞ If the current is moving at an average rate and the projection is slanting with the flow, an eddy will form on the downstream side (Diagram 4-A), causing the minerals to be caught behind it, especially if on an inside curve. This is termed a *suction eddy* because the backward and downward swirling current sucks the minerals behind the protrusion as it passes.

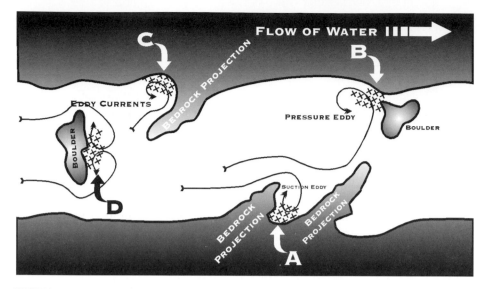

DIAGRAM 4 *Concentrations of heavy minerals caused by a suction eddy (A), a pressure eddy (B), an obstruction projecting against the current (C), and the downstream side of a large obstruction in a waterway (D).*

☞ The second case is created when the stream is moving rapidly. The projection, still slanting with the flow of water, will cause a crosscurrent, often creating what is called a *pressure eddy* (Diagram 4-B). This situation will force the heavy minerals to the opposite bank, where they may be held against the side by the resulting back swirl. It is particularly effective when there is an object, such as a large boulder, to further aid in the retention of the minerals.

☞ The third case is when the obstruction sticks into the stream against the current (Diagram 4-C). Here, if reaching out far enough, especially on an inner curve, it will trap any gemstones and other heavy minerals that hit it.

(6) Sand bars, whether near the bank or in the center of the stream are always suspect locations. If the bars are near the inner curves or if they interfere with an imaginary straight line drawn from one inner curve to the next, they are especially promising. The minerals, gold, and gemstones will, as was the case of the other obstructions, usually be found on the downstream side of such sand or gravel bars.

(7) The speed that a river is moving also plays an important role in whether or not anything is deposited. If it is moving too fast, it will erode the ground, carrying all minerals and everything else with it. Therefore, regions under very fast flowing water will not likely produce great concentrations of anything. Look for places where it is not moving exceptionally fast.

Remember that the basic rule for collecting in placer situations is the heavy minerals will sink when given the opportunity. Look for places which provide that opportunity.

□ PANNING

Panning is generally associated with finding gold, but it can also be useful for obtaining small pebbles of heavy gemstones such as sapphires, rubies, garnets, etc. (Photo 57)

When at a promising location, in a known producing region, always keep in mind that the theory behind panning and any other form of alluvial concentration is to settle or trap the heavy gold or other minerals to the bottom of the pan, through shaking, swirling and submerging in water, gradually removing the lighter material from the top. If you are looking for gemstones, be very sure you carefully examine any pebble you intend to discard before doing so. Sometimes a potentially valuable chunk of gravel will be so abraded that its true nature might be hidden beneath a severely roughed-up exterior.

The procedure for panning is not difficult, and, with a little practice, the necessary skill can easily be learned. Once you have obtained a gold pan and have prepared it, if necessary, according to the manufacturer's instructions, fill it about one-half to three-quarters full of sand and gravel from the chosen spot. Dig down as deep as possible, preferably to bedrock, since very little of the heavier minerals will be in the upper levels of mud. Sometimes a small hand trowel is useful for getting down to bedrock. Be careful, though, and don't allow much material to escape, since it might contain gems or gold. Be sure to also place anything found in cracks or other irregularities into the pan. It might be necessary to use a long screwdriver or a suction device to get it, but the extra time and effort might pay off.

PHOTO 57 *Panning for gold.*

Upon filling up with the prescribed amount of mud and gravel, it is time to start. The first thing to do is submerge the dirt laden pan and shake, trying to keep it as level as possible, not allowing anything but the lightest of materials to escape. Next, while the pan is still submerged, knead the soil to break up all clods that might be present. Any large stones should be rinsed in the upper levels of the pan and examined for gold or gemstone potential and either retained or discarded.

After having eliminated all of the large non-valuable stones and dissolving the dirt clods and clay, grip the pan, with both hands and again agitate it, trying to settle the heavier materials and allowing some of the lighter to escape out the top. Take your finger and stir, to further dissolve anything that may have been missed. Again, shake the pan, still slightly underwater. This time, however, in more of a circular motion. The centrifugal force, as well as the agitation, will cause the lighter substances to flow over the edge while the gold and heavy minerals will sink. Continue to remove the larger gravel after carefully examining it for potential value.

PHOTO 58 *Grip pan toward rear and dip into water away from you at a slight angle.*

By now, any gemstones and nuggets of worthwhile size have been picked out and all that remains is fine gold and tiny grains of other heavy minerals. Continue by gripping the pan toward the rear (nearest you) and dipping it into the water away from you at a slight angle (Photo 58). Move it in a circular motion, giving a slight jerk as it swings toward the point furthest away. This circular motion, accompanied by the little thrust, will propel the lighter contents from the pan. Be very careful, though, to not over tilt or become unduly zealous in your jerking and circling. This has to be a gradual elimination of the lighter materials to allow the heavier ones to remain on the bottom and not be expelled. Every 30 seconds or so it is good idea to level the pan and again shake it, just to make sure that the heavier substances do remain on the bottom and are not being slowly worked up by this process.

Continue, with frequent inspections, especially when most of the soil has been removed. Eventually you will have worked it down to black sand and gold. The black sands are simply the other heavy minerals that were contained in the mud. These include magnetite, ilmenite, hematite, pyrite, marcasite, rutile, wolframite, zircon, and garnet, but none of which, at this stage, should be large enough to be of any interest to you as a collector.

Now, remove the pan from the water and closely examine what remains.

Extract any nuggets or suspicious pebbles that might be seen (don't get your hopes up, however), add a small quantity of water, and give it a swirl, trying to get the black sand to string out along the pan's inner edge. Closely examine the results, possibly using a magnifying lens. If there is gold, it should be found farther back, at the tail of the thin streak of black sands.

Do not get frustrated if you find nothing the first time. Review what you may have done wrong. Are you at a place where gold and/or heavy gemstones can accumulate? Are these minerals known to occur on this stream? Did you get all the way down to bedrock? Were you careful to keep the gold and/or gems in the pan at all times, or did you get impatient and just slosh everything out? Did you inspect the black sands carefully (often a magnifying glass is helpful) or were you only looking for unreasonably large nuggets or pebbles? These are just a few of the questions you should ask yourself if you have no success. Maybe the next time, you will learn from your mistakes and have better luck.

□ DESERT PLACERS

When searching desert washes, do exactly as you would if exploring streams. Look for gravel deposits, inside curves, large boulders, and other obstacles that would concentrate the heavy minerals when water did flow. Remember, when these heavy minerals were released from their place in the ground, even in the desert, they were usually transported by water during heavy rains. At times, dry creeks are rushing torrents and gold, gemstones and other heavy minerals are easily carried along in exactly the same manner as in a stream.

□ METAL DETECTORS

Metal detectors can often be used advantageously to locate conductive metallic minerals such as gold, silver, pyrite, galena, etc. in both secondary and primary deposits and, in the process, can also help to locate often nice associated minerals and crystals (see Photo 23 in Chapter 3). A metal detector does have limits, however. Use it in places where you know metallic minerals can be found or in geological settings where they are likely to occur. Be also warned that those metallic minerals must be of a size large enough and close enough to the surface to be detected.

There are many variables that cause problems with metal detectors, and one of the most troublesome is that of ground interference. It would be very simple if the only metals in the soil were gold, and maybe a little silver and other precious metals thrown in. Then there would be no problem. That seldom happens, though. In most highly mineralized regions there are often large quantities of uninteresting metals, usually iron ores, which will also cause a registration on a detector. In these cases, the receiver will pick up the signal from the mineralization in the ground, as well as that from gold or other such collectable minerals. With these combined signals, it is extremely difficult, and often impossible, to differentiate between them. This has led to the development of the ground canceling feature in most modern metal detectors. Basically, what this does is enable the user to make adjustments to the local ground conditions. In other words, you will take a reading from a "typical" section of the terrain and be able to adjust that reading out.

One more recent development in metal detectors has been the discovery that lower frequencies have better ground penetrating abilities than the previously used higher ones. Furthermore, there is less interference from undesirable ground mineralization at these frequencies, affording greater amplification with the deeper penetration. These new, very low frequency (VLF), TR type detectors are regarded as among the best for use in seeking gold and other highly conductive metals.

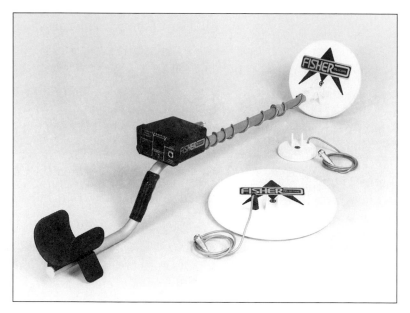

PHOTO 59 *A metal detector with small, medium, and large coils. Courtesy of Fisher Research Laboratory.*

Another important point that should be mentioned is searchcoil size. The large coils, over eight inches in diameter, are designed for detection of sizable metal objects, many feet below the surface. The smaller coils, three and one-half inch to five inch, concentrate their power to find smaller bits of metal, at more shallow depths (Photo 59).

□ LOCATIONS TO USE A METAL DETECTOR

On Mine Dumps

If you find an old abandoned prospect, there is a good chance that a metal detector may be useful in finding minerals, especially if it was associated with

94

precious metals or hydrothermal deposits.

The most efficient method for using a metal detector on a mine dump is to test individual chunks of rock and boulders, rather than simply sweeping the detector over the surface. There are usually so many interfering minerals on a mine dump that you would forever be getting conflicting signals.

To sample properly, place the metal detector on its side, with the coil propped up by a log or other nonmetal object. Next, take specimens and place them near the coil. If you get a positive response, more carefully inspect it by cracking and visually scrutinize a fresh surface for something of interest. Be advised that very uninteresting iron ores will also cause most metal detectors to register, so every specimen that you find may not be filled with beautiful shiny metallic minerals.

In Stream Placers

Metal detectors have been especially successful in helping find gold in streams. Be sure your detector has a waterproof searchcoil, then simply submerge it in places where you suspect the gold to be. If bedrock occurs far below the stream bed, a metal detector may not have much value in that particular waterway, since, the farther away the object is, the weaker the signal.

If a stream is known to produce metals, such as gold, and heavy gemstones, then the detector can be useful in locating pockets of both. Be advised, however, that gemstones are not conductive and will not cause a metal detector to register. Metal detectors can only be used to locate heavy gems when they are found together with conductive metals.

PHOTO 60 *Using a metal detector to survey potentially productive lands. Note traditional gold pan in the foreground. Photo courtesy of Garrett Metal Detectors.*

In the Field

When using a metal detector in the field for exploring such areas as bajadas or washes, conduct your search in a scientific manner, not just a random walk. Use a grid, or back and forth organized climb to survey everywhere (Photo 60). Don't overlap, but don't miss anything. Be alert for faint signals. If the signal is indistinct and in a rock face, try to determine whether the deposit continues in any direction or it emanates from a single source. You may be able to "follow" the signal to a spot where the orebody is either much larger, closer to the surface, or even an outcrop.

CHAPTER 9 LEGAL ASPECTS OF MINERAL COLLECTING

This chapter presents a little more detail than has already been provided relating to the laws and regulations governing rockhounding. Most who are reading this book will only be involved in recreational collecting, and full scale mining is not even a possibility. There is, however, a very slim chance that you might find mineralization valuable enough to at least consider filing a claim. For that reason, or if just curious, there is also a basic overview of what a claim involves, as well as the associated rights and responsibilities.

▢ THE BASICS

To review, you should always understand that you cannot just go anywhere in the country and start picking up rocks, digging, or even panning. Obviously, you can't pick up minerals on private property without the owner's permission and, in addition, there are many public lands that have been set aside by the government, whether local, state, or federal, which restrict or prohibit rock and mineral collecting. It is, therefore, a good idea to check with the district forest ranger, Bureau of Land Management, or other such governing body charged with the responsibility of overseeing any region in question to confirm what you can and cannot do.

We have already mentioned that you should always be certain that any mine dump upon which you plan to collect is abandoned and open to rockhounds. Sometimes, however, that is very difficult to do. The Bureau of Land Management (BLM) is currently working on a project of compiling a list of all mining claims on federal lands. The claims will be stored in a computer and there is a four-way, cross-reference system for checking on the current status of any particular prospect. If you can find the name of the owner, the name of the mine, the claim's serial number, or its geographical location (township, range, etc.), then that information can be fed into the computer and the status and other pertinent information will be located. If there is no record of the particular claim, then it is to be regarded as abandoned.

In addition to the BLM, some states are extremely efficient in recording claims within their boundaries, whether on federal or state land. Some even have mylar overlays which fit over standard topographic maps designating all claims and telling whether they are active or inactive. Obtaining such data before heading into the field can save many hours of backtracking and prevent getting yourself into awkward situations.

If your particular BLM office does not have up-to-date information on claim status, or if not researching federal land, you must resort to the old fashioned method of checking. This is done by taking a trip to the Country Recorder's office. It is quite an experience visiting many of these offices and often a real test of your patience and determination. The method of filing claims and assessment work information varies from recorder to recorder. I am personally convinced that there are annual competitions between them to determine who has the most archaic and unreasonable filing systems. I am also sure that I have been unlucky enough to visit most of the "winners" in this competition during the past few years. In any event, plan to spend many hours paging through volumes of records to determine the validity of a particular claim. The new BLM method of using computers and cross-reference systems should save lots of time.

□ CLAIMS

Most of the laws governing mining throughout the United States center around the basic mining law enacted in 1872. This is the foundation for state laws, as well as the federal counterparts. There are some variations and additional requirements, which differ from state to state, but these rights and requirements don't deviate drastically. In the following paragraphs is a summary of some of the most basic, but, in no way should they be construed as everything anyone needs to know about the legal aspects of mining and mineral rights. This is intended simply to provide a basic understanding of the subject. If you discover a potentially valuable mineral deposit, it is strongly suggested that you obtain a copy of the mining laws for the state within which you made your discovery and possibly consider consulting with a lawyer who specializes in mining law.

After a prospector has made a discovery of potential value, is certain that mining is allowed at the location, made sure that the discovery is not on somebody else's claim or on restricted or closed property, and feels it is worth the effort to pursue investing time and money, it is time to stake a claim. This gives certain rights, including the right to obtain minerals within the claim's physical boundaries and to use as much of the surface resources, such as trees, as is necessary to carry out the mining operation. The claimholder does not, however, possess surface rights; he or she only has the sole freedom to work the area for precious minerals without interference from others.

Interestingly, in some states you need not actually have made a discovery of precious minerals in order to gain mining rights to the land. In some situations, you can stake a claim if there is a reasonable suspicion that something of value is on the property. This is called a prospecting site and gives the claimholder exclusive rights to search for valuable minerals at that location without being bothered by others. When valuable minerals are found, a discovery post is erected and it is then changed to an actual mining claim.

It is necessary for a claimholder to annually put at least $100 worth of work into each of his or her claims, but that amount can vary upward, from state to state. This is called annual assessment work and must be done in the actual process of mining, not for building a summer cabin or clearing weeds from the property. Tools and transportation of tools or personnel to and from the mine cannot be used for assessment work either. Some states have additional requirements and restrictions. If the assessment work is not completed and proof filed every year, the claimholder may loose rights to the claim.

If a mine proves to be very productive and the claimholder wants to have full ownership rights, a patent can be applied for. In such cases, the claimholder actually owns the land and has surface rights as well as mineral rights to the property, just as any other private land owner.

In order to patent a mining claim, $500 worth of approved work must have taken place and proof of a worthwhile mineral discovery must be submitted, since there has been a long history of abuse of this privilege. In the past, and even currently, people have applied for and received patents on property where they have no intention of actually doing any mining. They fraudulently acquire the land in order to construct summer cottages or to make shrewd land investments. Because of this abuse, patents are becoming tougher to obtain, and proof is required that the mine is really productive.

Once a patent has been approved, the land is then purchased from the government for $2.50 an acre, for placer claims, and $5.00 an acre for lode claims. When the land has been purchased, there are no additional restrictions on it and the claimholder can do with it whatever they wish. They must, however, incur the cost of having it surveyed.

Any person can stake a claim and any number can be staked, as long as the required assessment work is done on each. There are no age requirements. The only real restriction is that a citizen of a foreign country may not obtain a patent unless first declaring an intention to become a citizen of the United States.

On federal public domain lands, there are two basic types of mining claims that can be staked. These are placers and lodes (secondary deposits and primary deposits). Before filing either type, though, you obviously must have discovered valuable minerals and there must be enough potential so that, as the law says, ". . . a normally prudent man would be encouraged to expend time and money in hopes of developing a profitable mine."

Placer Claims

Placer claims can be up to twenty acres each and usually measure 1320 feet by 660 feet. The dimensions may vary, but can be no more than twenty acres and the length no more than 1320 feet (Diagram 5). Whenever possible, a placer should correspond to the legal subdivision method of pinpointing pieces of land, using reference to a specific meridian and its associated townships, ranges, sections, etc. Therefore, the boundary lines, whenever possible, should run in north-south and east-west directions.

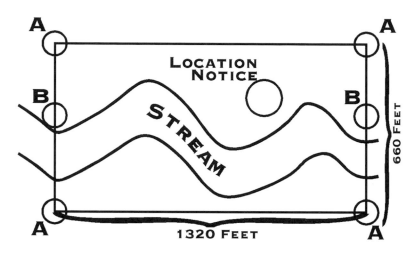

DIAGRAM 5 *The standard placer claim.*

A location notice should be posted near where the original discovery was made, in a conspicuous area on a discovery post, tree, or large rock. This notice should give the name(s) of the claimholder(s), the date of discovery, as well as the dimensions, area and compass directions. Also, a reference should be made to some permanent object such as a road, large boulder, river fork, etc.

A post or stone monument should also be placed at each corner (labeled A on Diagram 5), and most states also require center posts on the endlines (labeled B on Diagram 5). An attempt should be made to mark or brush out the boundary lines on the ground so that they can easily be seen by others. It is not necessary to erect the corner and center posts at the same time as the discovery post, but there are time limitations which vary from state to state governing how much time can elapse until they must be constructed.

A copy of the location notice is taken to the County Recorder's office within the amount of time specified by the particular state. It is also required, if the claim is on federal land, to record it with the Bureau of Land Management, to be entered into their computers, as previously mentioned. Some states have additional filing requirements. A fee is then paid to each of the agencies for recording the claim.

On federal lands, a group of people can get together and claim adjacent locations of twenty acres each, this being recorded as a single claim, called an association claim. It is limited to eight people, or a maximum of 160 acres, and there are some benefits to staking such a joint claim, the most important of which is that only one initial discovery is necessary, not eight.

100

Lode Claims

In contrast to placers, lode claims cannot be any longer than 1500 feet along the vein and cannot go more than 300 feet from the vein on either side. They are usually shaped like parallelograms (opposite sides parallel and equal in length). That means that the maximum size of a lode claim is 1500 feet by 600 feet with the vein running through it lengthwise. Diagram 6 illustrates the layout of a "typical" lode claim and Diagrams 7, 8, 9, and 10 show some variations. An attempt is usually made to make the end lines parallel so, in the future, if the claimholder wishes to have rights to follow the vein, if it happens to wander out of the originally staked boundaries, it can easily be done. These are called extralateral rights, and are often used, since most veins do not go in an absolute straight line.

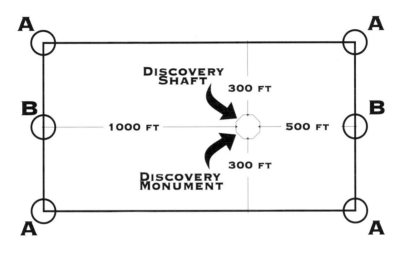

DIAGRAM 6 *The standard lode claim.*

As was the case with placers, posts should be constructed at the four corners (labeled A on Diagram 6), a location notice should be as close to the actual discovery shaft as possible, and most states also require center posts on the endlines (labeled B on Diagram 6). In some states, the discovery notice can be placed in the northeast corner, rather than having the fifth post, and an attempt should be made to mark or brush out the boundary lines.

The corner posts for both lodes and placers should be large enough to easily be seen and most states prescribe minimum heights and diameters. If wooden, they should be square and marked with the corner number or location, and a designation should be made as to the distance and direction to the next corner marker. If unable to obtain lumber, a pile of rocks, at the prescribed heights, is acceptable. Location and other pertinent information should be in a protective container within each of the monuments.

In some lodes it is impossible, due to the ruggedness of the terrain, to place a corner post exactly on the corner. In these cases, witness posts may be used. These are posts close to where the actual corner should be, and designate, in writing, the direction and distance to the associated corner, in addition to any other information that would have been on the actual corner post.

☐ VARIATIONS ON A STANDARD LODE CLAIM

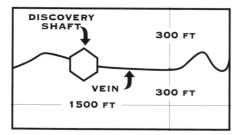

DIAGRAM 7 *Typical variation.*

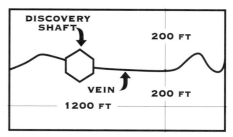

DIAGRAM 8 *Non-standard dimensions.*

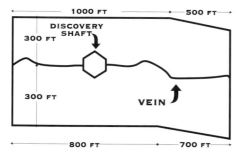

DIAGRAM 9 *Following an irregular vein.*

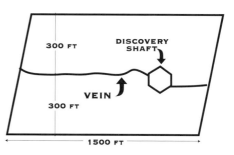

DIAGRAM 10 *Parallelogram model.*

CHAPTER 10 PREPARATION & PRESERVATION

When you get home from a collecting trip, accompanied by all the mineralogical treasures that were found, there will most likely be a profound realization that your specimens just aren't as nice as those you have seen in photographs or mineral stores. A few, though, might have some promise. There are some things that can and should be done to maximize the desirability of your finds, however, and this chapter will guide you through them.

What you collect on a field trip will probably fall into one of two distinctly different categories, crystallized specimens or cutting materials. The cutting materials are solid, massive minerals which, when shaped and polished, can be used for jewelry, carvings, bookends, spheres, and other such objects. They include chalcedony, agate, jasper, onyx, marble, rhyolite and a host of other micro-grained minerals and rocks. The most desirable cutting materials are those that exhibit lots of color and/or interesting patterns.

Crystallized specimens, on the other hand, are usually not polished, but, instead, simply cleaned, trimmed, and then displayed, just as they were formed in nature, to show their inherent natural beauty. This chapter deals primarily with how to best prepare and exhibit crystallized specimens. A detailed discussion of cutting materials will be deferred to Chapter 11.

Important warning: If you have any doubt your particular mineral(s) may be damaged by any process or procedure described in this chapter, it is a good idea to conduct a test on an already damaged surface or undesirable piece of exactly the same substance, just to be safe. Be sure to also pay particularly close attention to the warnings and cautions! A little advance research, as well as common sense, are the most essential prerequisites for determining how to clean and prepare any given mineral.

□ CLEANING

Cleaning is usually the first thing you do with specimens after getting them home. Cleaning not only provides the opportunity to better evaluate your finds, but it helps determine what to keep and what to consider getting rid of. The best way to clean most minerals is to simply squirt them with a garden hose. If they are fragile or if the particular mineral is water soluble, however, that wouldn't be such a good idea.

Clay is especially tough to remove from crystals, and a high pressure spray might be needed if the specimens are not too fragile. Ammonia mixed with water is also good for helping to get rid of especially persistent and sticky clay. Soak specimens in an amonia/water-filled bucket for a few hours and then spray. The procedure might have to be repeated a few times, but it usually does the job.

If you are still having trouble getting dirt and clay off specimens, try using dental tools, nails, or even stiff wire in order to get into tricky places (Photo 61). Just be sure that you don't do this on soft minerals that will be scratched by these instruments.

PHOTO 61 *Carefully cleaning a specimen.*

If still not adequately cleaned, try submerging the specimen in warm, but not hot, water and scrubbing with a toothbrush. Obviously, if you are dealing with delicate little crystals this is not a workable solution, but for most minerals it will do just fine.

Below are listed some additional warnings and suggestions related to cleaning mineral specimens. Always keep in mind that you, the collector, have the ultimate responsibility of determining whether or not it is damaging or safe.

☞ Never dip minerals into extremely hot or extremely cold water. Such quick temperature changes can cause them to fracture or shatter.

☞ Dry specimens as soon as possible after cleaning. Some minerals, such as pyrite and marcasite, start to tarnish almost immediately when wet and exposed to the air.

☞ Do not use any type of scouring powder unless certain the mineral being cleaned is harder than the powder. Severe damage could be done to soft minerals such as selenite.

☞ As mentioned earlier, do not use water, even lightly, on minerals that will be dissolved, such as halite or hanksite.

☞ If trying to clean an especially delicate mineral, it might be impossible to do anything more than lightly blow off the dust. A small electric blower can sometimes be used, but be very careful and pay close attention to how the mineral is reacting.

☞ If cleaning something porous, it is usually not a good idea to submerge it in any liquid. Try dry brushing with a paintbrush (Photo 62) or, as above, simply blow off the dust.

PHOTO 62 *Some minerals can be cleaned with a paintbrush.*

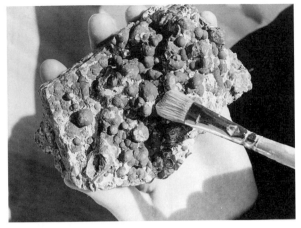

☞ A fairly good way to clean small crystals and gemstones is to place them into a screening frame and dip it into and out of a tub filled with water. Don't be too aggressive, though, since damage may be done. If any clay is left, try using a toothbrush to finish the job.

☞ There are ultrasonic cleaners on the market which can be very effective in cleaning some gemstones. If you use one, only do so with minerals known to be compatible with the process. Certain gemstones will shatter, crack, or otherwise be damaged when submitted to the ultrasonic waves. An ultrasonic cleaner is even more effective if the gemstones are submerged in detergent, ammonia, or diluted acid. Be very certain, however, to read all instructions and know your minerals before using any such agents.

☞ Very hardy minerals, especially agates, chalcedonys, and jaspers, can be cleaned by light tumbling. See Chapter 11 for specific details.

☞ There are a variety of small cleaning and buffing implements on the market which can be used with rotary devices such as small drills and flexible shaft carving machines. They should only be utilized on tough minerals, however, since the potential for damage is high.

☞ Bleach is often helpful in cleaning up calcium carbonates such as calcite, limestone, marble, and onyx. The bleach not only brightens up the color but it also removes minor stains.

PHOTO 63 *A variety of small implements which can be attached to small drills and flexible shaft carving machines for cleaning hard minerals.*

Acid Cleaning

A very effective way to clean many minerals is through the use of acids. It is imperative, however, that you first do some prudent research related to what type acid will effectively remove the particular stain from whatever mineral you are trying to clean. It must be able to devour the undesirable substance(s) while, at the same time, do no damage to the underlying mineral. This can get tricky. When in doubt, be sure to conduct a test on something you don't mind losing.

Many books on mineral identification will note a particular mineral's susceptibility to acids, but, if you cannot obtain such a publication, consider consulting a local lapidary or gem and mineral society, a museum, or even a professional dealer for guidance. Keep in mind that many minerals can't be cleaned with acid since they will be severely damaged.

While on the subject, it is important to note that when diluting acids, **always add acid to water** and not the other way around. When water is added to acid, it can cause a reaction accompanied by splattering. In addition, do not even consider using acid treatments unless you are willing to set up an appropriate and safe working area and follow proper procedures.

When you have finished using any acid, be sure to properly neutralize it. This can be done by simply dropping a few chunks of marble or limestone into the solution and waiting until all bubbling has ceased. The completely neutralized acid can then be poured into a drain for disposal.

Oxalic acid is relatively mild and probably the best choice for beginners. It can be purchased at some paint and hardware stores and is most commonly used to remove red and orange rust and limonite stains from quartz crystals, but it is not appropriate for cleaning calcium carbonates such as calcite, limestone, marble, and onyx. The process requires a week or more, but the results can sometimes be spectacular.

To prepare an oxalic acid bath, first dissolve 2-3 tablespoons of acid crystals in a gallon of warm, but not hot, water. Put the specimens in an aluminum or other type of acid resistant pan and then carefully pour in the acid solution until the crystals are completely submerged. Be sure to cover the container, not only to deter vapors from being emitted into the air, but also to prevent animals from drinking it.

If your specimens are not too delicate, you can speed up the procedure by periodically brushing or wiping off the softened but not yet completely dissolved stains every few days. If wiping with a rag or paper towel doesn't completely clean the crystal(s), at least the acid will be left with lots less to dissolve. When brushing or wiping an acid-bearing crystal, wear a pair of thick rubber gloves. If acid should get on your skin or clothes, immediately wash it off. Even oxalic acid can cause skin irritation if not promptly rinsed away.

Another way to speed up the cleaning process is to heat the crystal-bearing oxalic acid, if the minerals can handle it. Do not heat acid inside your home, do it outside by placing the container on a portable heating pad. If the solution starts to boil, be very careful. Not only can the acid splatter, but the crystals could crack. In addition, do not boil anything for more than fifteen or twenty minutes. If you have any concerns that the minerals you are treating may be susceptible to heat, be patient and only use the cool acid, even if the process takes many weeks.

When the specimens are clean, you should thoroughly wash them in soapy water, followed by a rinse. Allow them to completely dry before storage or display.

Hydrochloric acid can also be used for removing rust and limonite stains, and it works much faster than oxalic acid, but, consequently, is far more hazardous to use. If hydrochloric acid gets on your skin or clothing it could be painful and damaging. If it gets in your eyes, there could be a major problem. Only use hydrochloric acid if you know what you are doing and are willing to follow all safety precautions.

When using hydrochloric acid, you will almost immediately see the chemical reaction, resulting in dark yellow clouds swirling throughout the solution until it turns almost red. Quartz crystals can often be completely cleaned in less than an hour, in contrast to many days or weeks with oxalic acid. Hydrochloric acid is also very helpful in removing carbonates such as calcium and limestone from acid resistant minerals. Bubbles will immediately start to emanate from the carbonates and, when they stop, all will have been completely dissolved away.

Do not use hydrochloric acid to clean azurite, calcite, chrysocolla, fluorite, galena, garnet, gypsum, halite, hematite, malachite, marble, or serpentine, since such minerals will be quickly damaged.

Glacial acetic acid can also be used to remove calcite and other carbonates from acid resistant crystals. It can be obtained from most photo supply stores, and works much slower than hydrochloric acid, thereby providing more safety and control.

□ TRIMMING

Trimming, beyond what was done in the field to reduce the specimen to a manageable size, is usually the second step in mineral preparation. The reasons a collector would want to make a specimen smaller are many. First, size is not the overriding benchmark of value or desirability. Instead, it is quality. Specimens should be carefully cut down to get rid of any distracting matrix or damaged crystals, thereby leaving only the finest portions. Beautiful crystals and/or bright, interesting colors and patterns can be lost within large and otherwise unsightly native rock.

It is not as easy as you might first expect to trim your finds. Potentially spectacular specimens can be ruined by careless attempts at trimming. In fact, even the most skilled collector will occasionally damage what would have been a nice specimen. There might be hidden fractures which will separate without warning or a crystal might just shatter or break off for no apparent reason when the piece is struck in just the right (or wrong) way.

Different types of rocks break in many different ways. Some stone is very tough and easy to trim, but other stones are quite susceptible to internal fracture or breakage. It is strongly suggested that you spend some time experimenting on poor quality samples before trying to trim something with great potential, just to see what happens.

If what you are working on is tough, then trimming can probably be accomplished by using a sharp cold chisel and hammer. Just take your time. Carefully place the chisel at the appropriate place, away from existing fractures, and give it a quick, sharp strike with the hammer. Sometimes placing the specimen on a block of wood or in a pile of rags is helpful in order to reduce the internal shock.

If your specimen is very delicate or it just won't break off the way you want with a cold chisel and hammer, other types of tools should be considered. There are chisel-edged hammers, rock nippers, pliers with wide-edged ends, and even specially designed vice-like rock trimmers. Rock trimmers look like little screw presses with chisel like jaws (Photo 64). The specimen is lined up so the jaws will cut at the desired spot and then it is tightened. Hydraulically powered models are also available, being far more powerful, generally much larger, and, as you might expect, much more expensive.

If the specimen is so delicate that none of the tools mentioned above will work, then the undesirable sections can be sawed off with a diamond saw, as discussed in the next chapter. Keep in mind, though, that specimens tend to be more valuable and look better in collections with "natural" rather than clean cut edges. Sometimes, however, the choice is unavoidable and a saw must be used.

If you do use a diamond saw to trim a specimen, there are a few words of advice. First, try to cut in regions which will be less visible when displayed, in an effort to preserve as much of the natural appearance as possible. Secondly, be careful when se-

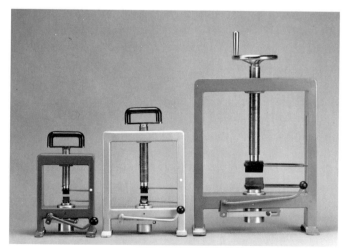

PHOTO 64 *A selection of rock trimmers. Courtesy of the Wydar Company.*

lecting what type lubricant to use. Diamond saw coolant is usually oil based and can stain or otherwise damage some minerals. Most can be cleaned off with warm water and dish soap, but do your research beforehand in order to prevent disappointing consequences.

□ CATALOGUING

You should always temporarily label your specimens and try to properly identify them while still in the field. Wrap them with a numbered slip of paper or attach white tape marked with a number corresponding to its descriptive counterpart in a notebook. The notebook should contain such information as tentative identity, where it was found, and when it was found. The notations might also include a rough sketch of the piece, and other pertinent information such as the name of any associated mine, guidebook used to located the mineral (if applicable), distinguishing characteristics, etc. If it is especially nice, a few color photos, also catalogued in your notebook, not only of the specimen itself, but also the location of discovery and surrounding terrain might prove to be helpful at a later time.

When you get home, even before cleaning your specimens, it is a good idea to first make sure you know which mineral is which. If the marking tape has come loose or the numbered slip of paper is lost, it is still likely you can piece things together by referring to the notebook.

After cleaning and trimming, it is a good idea to give your minerals a permanent reference number. The best way to do this is to paint a small white spot, about one inch in diameter, on some uninteresting portion, most often the bottom. When the paint is dry, use an ultra-fine-tip, permanent, ink marker or an India ink pen to carefully place a number on the white area (Photo 65). Do not use a number already used, and be sure to keep a catalogue of minerals, numerically, in a notebook and/or a computer database. The computer is an excellent way to store mineral information and, if set up properly, information can be sorted just about any way you want. You can have a numerical listing, a listing by mineral name, list by location found, etc., etc.

PHOTO 65 *Numbering on the back of a mineral specimen.*

□ DISPLAY

As you pursue mineral collecting, you will surely want to display some of your finest specimens. They might represent an especially enjoyable trip, be unusually well crystallized, or exhibit exceptional colors. Whatever your reasons for selection, you want them to be presented the best way possible. Advanced collectors either purchase or build nice display cabinets (Photos 66 & 67), while most amateur collectors simply show choice pieces on open shelves or in knickknack cabinets.

If displayed on open shelves, unprotected from dust, cooking fumes, etc., be sure to keep them well cleaned. A dust buildup will conceal their true beauty. Do not over-clean, however. Every time you handle a delicate crystal there is a chance of damage. Distilled water is good for a relatively safe and mild cleaning of most minerals, but some specimens should only get a light dusting or blowing off.

Try not to overcrowd your shelves and display areas. Highlight only your best and/or most significant minerals. Don't let them get lost among lots of clutter. If you have too many minerals to properly show, either consider expanding your display areas or narrowing down to only the most prized of the prize pieces. The others can be conveniently stored in drawers or easily accessible boxes, ready for your own personal viewing or to show to anyone who expresses an interest.

PHOTO 66 *Two professionally made display cases. Courtesy of O'Brien Manufacturing.*

It is also important to spend some time determining exactly how to exhibit your minerals for the best impact and display of their beauty. Consider size, color, crystallization, etc., for balance and placement. Large rocks might be best on the bottom of cabinets or on the ends or rear portions of shelves. The smaller minerals would be better on the upper, more easily seen levels, or in front of the more sizable ones.

110

Sometimes some creativity will be needed in order to best display an awkward mineral that simply will not stay put. You obviously want the very finest portion of any specimen to be what is most easily seen. To help accomplish that task, it might be necessary to either construct or purchase pronged mineral holders and/or display easels. Nice, professionally made stands constructed from plastic or metal can be obtained at most lapidary or mineral supply stores. In some cases a glob of clay or wax can be used for support, but that usually isn't very attractive.

PHOTO 67 *A suggested method of displaying mineral specimens.*

Labels should also be made for your display case or for shelves upon which your prized specimens will be displayed. How much information is contained on those labels is up to your own personal preference. Seasoned collectors might want as much information as possible, while others may only want the mineral's name. A few suggested display labels are provided in Appendix A.

□ SOME SPECIAL CONSIDERATIONS

Where to store or display specimens is probably the most overlooked and, believe it or not, potentially the most important part of mineral preservation. Because of the somewhat slow process of weathering and chemical reactions, this is not usually considered to be overly important. Keep in mind, however, that many minerals were enclosed in airtight and temperature stable cavities, deep within the earth, since the time they were formed, and they might very well have trouble adapting to their new and more harsh environment. Remember that even a sturdy chunk of steel can rapidly deteriorate into rust if exposed to air and moisture, and the same is true of many minerals. Pyrite, iron, sphalerite, stibnite, realgar, marcasite and copper are easily tarnished or even completely decomposed just by exposure to oxygen.

It is interesting to note that there is often no consistency in how certain minerals deteriorate. The same mineral, found in different locations, may exhibit great variance in its susceptibility to decompose. A pyrite from one location might remain very stable in a collection, while a pyrite from a completely different locality could start to show signs of deterioration almost immediately and will need to be kept in a controlled environment to prevent complete destruction.

Here are some suggestions to consider before storing or displaying:

☞ Be certain your display cabinet doesn't contain heat-radiating light. Not only does heat speed up many chemical processes, it can also directly break down some minerals.

☞ Mineral incompatibility is another potential problem to consider. Some are just fine, except when displayed near certain others. Before setting up a display, it is a good idea to do some research on the subject. Sulfur is especially suspect in many cases. If you notice a slow deterioration of a particular mineral it could very well be that it is near another specimen emitting fumes that are destructive to it. Most minerals, however, are not affected this way.

☞ Sometimes continual exposure to light, even if not radiating heat, will cause surface reactions and deterioration, as is the case with beryl, tourmaline, fluorite, quartz, topaz, barite, and selenite. Colors in such minerals can actually fade when exposed to intense light.

☞ Another factor that could have a detrimental effect on some minerals is humidity. If stored in an extremely humid area, such minerals as halite will become wet and could actually dissolve. Placing silica-gel near such specimens will help to prevent such damage.

☞ To further complicate the situation, there are also minerals, such as some borax ores, that will become powdery and disintegrate if stored in very dry places. This is due to the loss of internal moisture and, in such situations, care should be taken in regard to where they are stored or displayed.

☞ Substantial shifts in temperature can crack some minerals including fluorite, opal, and sulfur. Freezing weather can actually fracture anything that might contain internal pockets of water, such is occasionally encountered in beryl, calcite, quartz, gypsum and halite.

The decomposition factors discussed here do not affect most minerals and, if common sense and care is used for display and storage, any deterioration or discoloration will be minimal or nonexistent.

□ PACKAGING

Minerals not stored in display cabinets should be placed carefully in drawers or sturdy boxes. If boxed, they should be wrapped for protection in tissue paper, cotton, or something other than newspaper, which tends to deteriorate rapidly. There are also plastic or glass vials, see through zip-lock bags, and even specially made mineral storage boxes available from lapidary and mineral supply stores, any of which should suffice.

CHAPTER 11 CUTTING & POLISHING

A lapidary is a person engaged in cutting, shaping, and polishing stones. That craft, also referred to as lapidary, is a natural complement to mineral collecting. It is a rare rockhound who doesn't eventually get involved in some way. This chapter serves as an introduction to working with cutting materials, those solid, fine-grained stones capable of withstanding the stresses associated with being cut and polished. Such minerals include chalcedony, agate, jade, jasper, onyx, marble, rhyolite, serpentine, and most precious gemstones, and it doesn't take a lot of artistic talent to get started.

Advanced aspects of the lapidary craft can take years to master, even at the most basic levels, but many skilled craftsmen make a nice supplementary income by selling what they make at craft fairs, swap meets, gem and mineral shows, or through professional dealers. That usually is not the primary motivating factor, however. For most, it is simply the enjoyment of taking a rather common appearing stone and turning it into something beautiful.

It is possible to spend considerable sums of money on lapidary equipment, but the most basic elements of the craft don't require much of an investment at all. Start with the minimum and gradually expand, as your interest and skills develop.

The projects discussed on the following pages are not presented as complete and thorough instructions. They are furnished to get you started and to provide a fundamental understanding about what is involved. If your interest is stimulated, which might just happen, consider taking some classes through a local lapidary club or shop, and/or purchasing a good book specifically devoted to whatever aspect(s) of lapidary you want to pursue.

□ TUMBLING

Tumbled stones, sometimes referred to as baroque stones, are small, irregularly rounded, polished pebbles. Their smooth and glossy surfaces are produced by using mechanically powered, rotating drums called tumblers (Photo 68). The theory behind tumblers is modeled after nature's smoothing and rough polishing of river stones. They do the job considerably faster, however, by using very hard abrasives, called grits, instead of sand and gravel. The coarseness and toughness of the grits can be carefully controlled in order to ultimately place a near glass-like surface on the stones. By starting with a very coarse and highly abrasive grit, the rough edges can be quickly broken down and smoothed. Then, progressively finer and finer abrasives can get rid of scratches and other imperfections.

PHOTO 68 *A standard rotary tumbler and (left) and a vibrating tumbler (right). Photo courtesy of Tru-Square Metal Products.*

Grits are packaged according to coarseness, designated by a number associated with the grain size. The lower the number, the more coarse and destructive it will be. For tumbling purposes, an 80 grade grit is generally the most abrasive, while 600 grade is the finest (Photo 69). Grit is usually sold by the pound, the cost is reasonable, and it can be obtained at most lapidary supply stores or through catalogues.

If you want to try your hand at tumbling, start with a small, inexpensive rotary machine consisting of a motor, rollers, and at least one barrel to hold your stones (see Photo 68). In addition, secure a pound each of 80-, 220-, 400- and 600-grade grit, as well as some powdered polish.

PHOTO 69 *Packages of grit, polish, and pellets which are sometimes added to tumblers.*

114

Once the equipment and supplies are ready, it is necessary to select exactly which stones you want to polish. It is best to start with agate and jasper, since they are hard, somewhat forgiving to small mistakes, and they take a brilliant polish. Whatever you choose, however, should be about the same size and hardness. Until you develop some skill, try to avoid minerals softer than 5.0 on the Mohs Scale. Be sure to also shun anything that appears flaky, cracked, or severely pitted, since such stones will probably produce disappointing results.

Thoroughly wash your stones and fill the barrel approximately two-thirds full. Sprinkle in the proper amount of 80-grade grit (determined by the size of your tumbling barrel) and add enough water to cover everything. Securely fasten the lid, place it on the rollers, and turn on the power. The barrel should be allowed to rotate between seven and ten days, depending upon the hardness and roughness of the stones, but it is a good idea to occasionally open the barrel and evaluate progress. This serves two purposes. First, it allows you to see how things are going, and, second, removing the lid lets any gasses that may have accumulated inside the barrel escape. A rare, but messy problem associated with tumbling, is that gas sometimes builds up due to chemical reactions and the lid can actually be popped off, spilling gritty "mud" and partially tumbled stones everywhere.

After your stones have been completely smoothed, with all jagged edges removed, it is time to change to a finer grit. The most fundamental rule for tumbling is that whenever you change grits, it is essential that you completely clean off all coarse material before adding something finer. If just a few particles of the more coarse grit are left on the stones or in the barrel, they will cause scratches that cannot be removed during later stages of the process.

Put the freshly cleaned stones back into the freshly cleaned barrel, sprinkle in the prescribed amount of the next finest grit, in this case 220 grade, and cover with water, as before. Turn on the machine for another seven to ten days, inspecting periodically. Repeat the process of cleaning and refilling with the 400-grade and then the 600-grade abrasives.

Once the stones have completed their tumble in the 600-grade grit, they should have a shiny, silky appearance and be ready for polishing. The most common types of polish are cerium oxide and chrome oxide, but there are others which are as good or, in some cases, even better, especially when working with more tricky or fragile minerals. Place the thoroughly washed stones back into the barrel, add the prescribed amount of polish, cover with water, and start up the tumbler. The stones should be allowed to continuously tumble in the polish mix for at least three days, being examined periodically, as before. When the stones exhibit a mirror finish on a dry surface, they are ready for washing in a mild detergent. It is important to mention that when evaluating any polished stone, the best assessment is done by inspecting a dry surface, since small scratches and other flaws are difficult or impossible to detect when wet.

The most common type of tumblers are standard rotary models, but another popular design is the vibrator. Vibrating tumblers do not have a rotating barrel, but, instead, the container is stationary, and just shakes (see Photo 68). The vibrations cause the stones to move about and be subsequently ground and smoothed by the grits and polish in exactly the same way as a standard tumbler. Vibrating tumblers tend to be a little quicker, but either type does a good job.

□ DIAMOND SAWS

A basic step necessary for the production of most lapidary objects is the ability to saw through rock. To accomplish that task, craftsmen use what is referred to as a diamond saw. Such a device features a circular blade whose rim is impregnated with industrial grade diamond chips (Photo 70). Rock, unlike wood on a standard saw, however, cuts very slowly. Large pieces of hard agates and jaspers might take many hours or even days to completely cut through, while small pieces of soft minerals may be sliced almost as fast as a carpenter cuts through a chunk of lumber.

PHOTO 70 *A selection of diamond blades. Courtesy of Raytech Industries, Inc.*

A diamond saw is essential if you plan to progress past tumbling, and basic models are relatively inexpensive. Small trim saws (Photo 71) are used just as a standard table saw. Their blades generally measure from 4 inches to 6 inches in diameter and the piece of rock is fed through by hand pressure. Large saws, with blades measuring eighteen inches in diameter or more, are needed when cutting large chunks of stone for use as clock faces, bookends or other such sizable objects (Photo 72). Since it takes so long for the larger rocks to be cut, the big machines are usually equipped with some sort of automatic feeding system.

Heat buildup is an important factor to be dealt with in just about any aspect of cutting and sawing of rock. Blades can be ruined and rock fractured if the temperature is allowed to get too high. Most lapidary equipment has

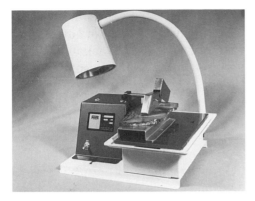

PHOTO 71 *A small 4" diamond trim saw. Photo courtesy of Raytech Industries, Inc.*

PHOTO 72 *A large table model 18" diamond saw. Photo courtesy of Raytech Industries, Inc.*

been designed with some means of supplying a liquid coolant to areas being cut, in order to keep the temperature under control. The type of coolant you use depends upon many factors. If you are only operating a small trim saw on thin and somewhat soft minerals, water might be acceptable. If, however, you are cutting large and/or very hard stones, where the heat has time to build up, it is necessary to use something more effective. Contact the saw manufacturer or dealer from whom you purchased your equipment for additional advice on the best way to proceed. Be very careful if you intend to cut porous stones, since oil based coolants can soak in and permanently discolor them.

DRILLING

Many jewelry applications require that a gemstone has a hole drilled into or through it. Drilling such a hole has been made quite simple by the advent of high speed diamond drills and small drill presses (Photo 73).

A diamond impregnated drill can cut through a stone quite rapidly, but they tend to be somewhat fragile and must be treated with care. The drill is attached to a variable speed motor which is controlled by a rheostat peddle switch. It is advisable that beginners start with one of a large diameter, since they are less likely to bend or break. Then, as you develop the "touch," smaller, more fragile and delicate drills can be used.

To make a hole in a gemstone, place the piece directly below the drill and either firmly hold it with your hands or embed it in putty or clay to keep it from moving. Start the drilling by gently lowering the diamond tip onto the top of the stone at exactly the place where you want the hole. Continually add

117

and release pressure so the coolant can flow to the drill tip. A good way to keep the temperature reasonable is to place the stone into a small pan or cup and completely cover it with coolant while being worked.

Most diamond drills are broken by either letting the tip get too hot or by applying undue pressure and bending the drill. Don't be impatient, since it takes a while to get completely through a hard stone.

PHOTO 73 *A small press for drilling holes into rocks. Courtesy of Covington Engineering.*

□ SHARPENING DIAMOND BLADES AND DRILLS

If your diamond saw blade or drill doesn't seem to cut as well as it did when new, it probably needs to be "sharpened" or dressed. Most likely, the diamonds have not been worn down, since they are much harder than whatever you have been drilling or cutting. What happens is that heat sometimes causes the encasing metal of the blade to slightly melt and cover the diamonds, thereby preventing their direct contact with the stone. The term dressing a drill bit or saw blade refers to removing that metal which covers the diamonds. In the case of a blade, the task is accomplished by sawing into an old grinding wheel. Just make some cuts into the old wheel and it will abrade the metal off the diamonds and render them useful again. To dress a diamond drill, run it into an old grinding wheel nine or ten times and, as was the case with the saw blade, the diamonds will be cleaned and ready for more work, just as if they were new.

□ CABOCHONS

Cabochons are probably the most common non-tumbled type of lapidary object produced by beginners, and the word is derived from the French term meaning "bald head." Basically, a cabochon has a flat bottom, domed top, and is either oval, round, square, or rectangular in shape. Cabochons can be extremely beautiful and worthy of setting into rings, bracelets, pins, pendants, and any number of other pieces of jewelry.

Just about any stone that will take a polish can be used for cabochons.

118

Transparent gemstones, however, are customarily reserved for faceting (to be discussed later in this chapter) in order to better show off their internal beauty and color. Opaque to translucent minerals such as chalcedony, agate, jasper, jade, onyx, rhodochrosite, and malachite, just to name a few, are the most popular cabochon materials. Agates and jaspers are probably the best to learn from since they are hard, often very colorful, and forgiving to mistakes. Other minerals may present problems for beginners. For example, jade either tends to flake or exhibit a rippled surface, and opal, if it gets too hot, will shatter. Turquoise and malachite are very soft, and too much pressure on the grinding wheel could create an immediate need to reduce size. Tiger eye and other asteriated or cat's-eye-type stones require special thought in regard to proper alignment before being cut so the special effects can be best presented. Tackling all these challenges comes with experience.

The theory behind grinding and polishing a cabochon is the same as with tumbling, except instead of using grits, you use graded grinding wheels, water resistant sandpapers, and, finally, the polish (Photo 74). Cabbing units can be quite small (Photo 75) to somewhat sizable (Photo 76), with the larger ones being more versatile in regard to the range of gemstone size, etc. The grinding wheels are either made of an abrasive stone-like compound or diamond impregnated aluminum, the latter being far more expensive but longer lasting and capable of producing more consistent results.

Throughout the entire cabbing process, everything must be kept cool, since heat buildup can crack the stone or damage the wheel. Most cabbing equipment is equipped with some means of supplying water to the cutting areas and how the task is accomplished might be a deciding factor related to what type machine you purchase.

PHOTO 74 *An all in one-unit which includes a trim saw, grinder, sander and polisher. Photo courtesy of Maxant Company.*

119

PHOTO 75 *An eight-inch grinder, sander, and polisher unit with a flexible and variable water spout. Courtesy of Crystalite Corporation.*

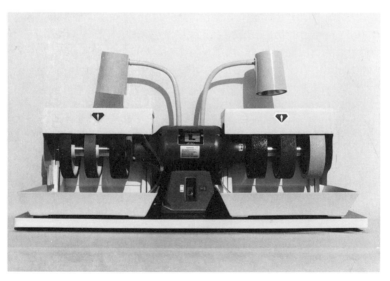

PHOTO 76 *A full-scale diamond wheel grinding and polishing unit. Courtesy of Diamond Pacific Tool Corporation.*

□ PROCEDURES FOR MAKING A CABOCHON

☞ If you want to fashion a cabochon, it is first necessary to use a diamond saw to cut a slab of whatever mineral you plan to use. The thickness of the slab will determine the maximum height of the final polished stone.

☞ Next, an outline of the outer cabochon circumference should be drawn onto the slab using a professionally made template which can be purchased

120

at any lapidary supply store. Templates are inexpensive and can be obtained with cutouts for all standard shapes and sizes. Select the exact size and shape you want, lay the appropriate template onto the slab so the most colorful and/ or most beautifully patterned region is completely within its boundaries, and then mark the outline with an aluminum pencil. Aluminum pencils can also be obtained at lapidary stores and are preferred over standard pencils since the marks are more permanent and won't be washed off.

☞ The next step in the manufacture of cabochons involves the use of a small diamond-bladed trim saw to cut around the outline. Since only straight cuts can be made with a trim saw, the edge will be ragged and approximate. Try to cut as much extra stone off as possible, in order to expedite the grinding process, but don't cut inside the lines (Diagram A).

☞ After the slab has been cut as close to the outline as practical, the blank, as it is called, is then adhered to a dop stick (usually a wooden dowel or cylindrical aluminum or plastic rod) with a specially formulated wax. The reason blanks are attached to dop sticks is to allow for better leverage and maneuverability during the shaping and polishing process. To attach them, the

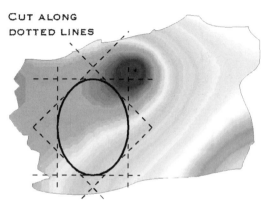

CUT ALONG DOTTED LINES

Diagram A *Cut your slab as close to the aluminum pencil outline of the proposed cabochon as you can with the trim saw.*

stick is first dipped into melted wax until it has a good, thick blob on the end, and then pressed onto the marked side of the gemstone blank (Diagram B). When the wax has cooled, the stone will be securely attached and shaping can continue.

☞ Grind the circumference of the blank to the exact shape originally marked onto the slab with the aluminum pencil. This is done using a 120-grade, coarse grinding wheel. Remember that it is important to not get inside the marked outline. Be sure to frequently check your stone in order keep track of where you are.

☞ When the blank has been shaped precisely to the outline, a bevel should be ground at an angle of about 45 degrees along the entire outside edge. Leave a small banded region at the bottom, still perpendicular to the base and preserving the shape (Diagram C). Keep in mind that if the bevel doesn't have a constant width and angle, your finished cabochon will end up lopsided, so take time to do it correctly.

☞ Once the first bevel is ground around the blank, tilt it a little more and make another bevel on top of the first, toward the top and center. Continue

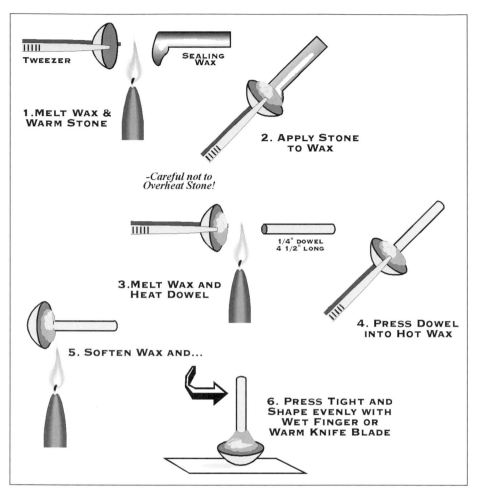

TWEEZER

SEALING WAX

1. MELT WAX & WARM STONE

2. APPLY STONE TO WAX

-Careful not to Overheat Stone!

3. MELT WAX AND HEAT DOWEL

1/4" DOWEL
4 1/2" LONG

4. PRESS DOWEL INTO HOT WAX

5. SOFTEN WAX AND...

6. PRESS TIGHT AND SHAPE EVENLY WITH WET FINGER OR WARM KNIFE BLADE

DIAGRAM B *The steps for mounting a stone onto a dop stick.*

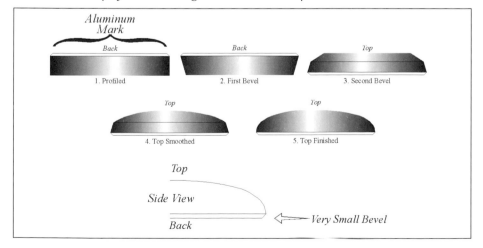

Aluminum Mark

Back

1. Profiled

Back

2. First Bevel

Top

3. Second Bevel

Top

4. Top Smoothed

Top

5. Top Finished

Top

Side View

Back ⟸ *Very Small Bevel*

DIAGRAM C *Side view showing the various steps involved to create a cabochon.*

this process two or three more times, as carefully and precisely as you can, until you have a step-like series of flat bevels running around the stone forming a crude, dome-shaped top.

☞ Next, you should gently and carefully rock the stone back and forth, all the way around, in order to smooth those rough beveled edges into a nice domed top (Diagram D). From time to time, throughout this critical forming process, stop your work, wipe off the stone and examine it for symmetry, smoothness, and shape. It is much easier to make modifications when using the coarse grinding wheel than by waiting until you are on a finer one. It is always frustrating to have to go back to a previous step because it wasn't done properly in the first place.

☞ When the cabochon has been completely formed and smoothed on the coarse wheel, clean everything to remove all residue from the previous step, and move to the finer 220-grade wheel. This is very much like the process of changing to progressively finer and finer grits in the tumbling process.

When finished with the 220-grade wheel, thoroughly wash the stone and dry it. If there are still some deep scratches or the dome is not yet perfectly rounded and symmetric, return to the 220 wheel to complete the task, since it will be impossible to correct those flaws later.

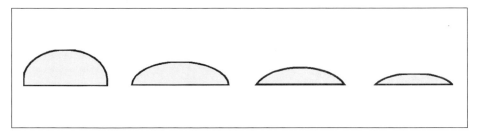

DIAGRAM D *Some side views of a typical cabochon.*

☞ Go next to the 220-grade sandpaper. Generally, cabbing machines are equipped with either a disk or drum sander, and water resistant sandpaper of appropriate grade is placed on its own individual holder. Some cabbing machines allow water to be squirted onto the rotating sandpaper wheel, just as was the case with grinding wheels, but others require that you continuously dip your stone into a small container of water to keep it cool. Whatever the case, do not let the stone overheat or it could crack and all will be lost!

☞ Proceed next to 400-grit sandpaper and continue removing scratches with a light touch and patience. Keep a clean rag nearby so you can periodically dry the stone in order to best assess progress.

☞ The 600-grade paper is next, and when that step is complete the dry stone will appear almost polished, emanating a slight silky sheen. Carefully inspect the cabochon for scratches, possibly even using a small magnifying lens.

PHOTO 77 *Rough chunk of malachite.*   PHOTO 78 *Cut slab of malachite.*

PHOTO 79 *Left to right: Slab with cabochon outlines, slab trimmed as close as possible to the outline with a trim saw, slab ground to the outline with a coarse grinder, slab with bevel made toward the top, slab after making a second and third bevel, the final polished cabochon.*

PHOTO 80 *Left to right: Premade setting, chain, and completed necklace.*

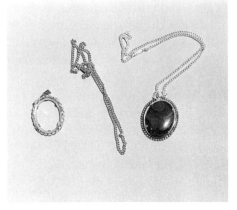

☞ If the stone is scratch-free, thoroughly clean everything. Place the polishing wheel or drum onto your cabbing machine, make some polishing paste by mixing powdered polish with water, smear the paste onto the polishing wheel, and work the stone against it as you did with the sandpaper. Depending upon the hardness of the stone, it won't take too long before a high-gloss finish is obtained. As before, keep the stone cool, stopping frequently to examine your progress by drying the stone and looking for dull spots that need more buffing.

☞ When done, your cabochon can be removed from the dop stick by either carefully heating it over a flame to melt the wax or by placing it into a freezer for a few minutes and just snapping it off. The freezing causes the wax to shrink, thereby releasing its grip. Excess wax which might still be left on the back of the stone can be scraped off with a knife.

□ FLAT POLISHING

For many projects such as clock faces, bookends, sliced geodes, nodules, or slabs, it is necessary to polish large flat surfaces. Polishing a flat surface is referred to as lapping and it is difficult, if not impossible, to do it on a curved grinding wheel. To help accomplish that task are vibrating and rotating lapping machines.

A vibrating lap works on the same principal as a vibrating tumbler. It consists of a flat metal tray placed on top of a base containing the motor. The stones are put flat side down onto the tray which has been smeared with grit and water (Photo 81). The coarse 80-grade grit is used first, followed by subsequently finer grits, until the process is completed using a polish. As was the case with tumbling, every time you change grits to a finer grade, it is imperative that equipment and stones are completely cleaned, leaving no trace of the more coarse abrasive.

In some cases, if the specimen to be polished is light in weight, a heavy object should be placed on top. The added weight will increase the effectiveness of the abrasive action. This is especially helpful when polishing slabs.

A rotating lap is similar to its vibrating counterpart, but, instead, the grit-bearing plate spins, and the flat side of the stone is held against it (Photo 82). A flat lap works much faster than a vibrating lap, because pressure is being

PHOTO 81 *A vibrating flat lap machine used to polish flat surfaces. Courtesy of Lortone.*

directly applied. The stone is moved back and forth on the rotating plate and is turned at all angles to the rotation in order to assure an evenly smoothed surface with no scratches or abrasion marks. Instead of using grit many modern flat laps use diamond-impregnated plates of varying coarseness or a diamond paste is smeared onto the metal wheel instead of the standard carborundum grits.

PHOTO 82 *A rotating flat lap machine. Courtesy of Gryphon Corporation.*

□ FACETING

The art of faceting encompasses some of the more advanced lapidary skills, but is briefly discussed here to provide an overview, since nearly all transparent gemstones such as diamonds, rubies, emeralds, and sapphires (Diagram E) are fashioned using this technique.

Faceted stones are similar to cabochons except, instead of having domed and curved surfaces, their entire surface is made up of little flat regions which are mathematically placed to best show the brilliance and internal color of the particular stone. Some gemstones are better cut with lots of facets or with facets in specific patterns or arrangements, while others produce more desirable results with a limited number. It all has to do with the internal reflections

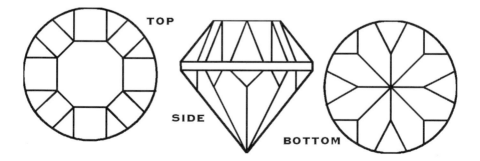

Diagram E *A typical faceted stone.*

inherent with each type stone and the associated visual results.

The theory behind making a faceted stone is very similar to that governing the production of a cabochon. You start with a coarse grind and work your way down to the polish. The mathematically arranged flat surfaces (facets) are placed on the gemstone with a faceting machine (Photo 83), but, as just mentioned, the procedure requires considerably more patience and skill than with cabochons (Photo 84).

PHOTO 83 *A faceting machine with gravity feed water supply. Courtesy of Jarvi Tool Company / Facetron.*

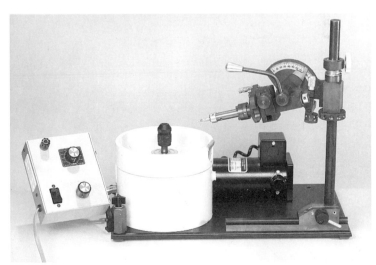

PHOTO 84 *A faceting unit with a good view of the facet head and various calibration scales. Courtesy of Poly-Metric Instruments.*

The first step in faceting is to determine exactly how the particular gemstone would best be cut. There are countless books written on the subject, and most contain literally hundreds of different designs (Diagram F), each with its unique benefits and shortcomings. Accompanying each design are diagrams and formulas for determining exactly where each facet should be placed.

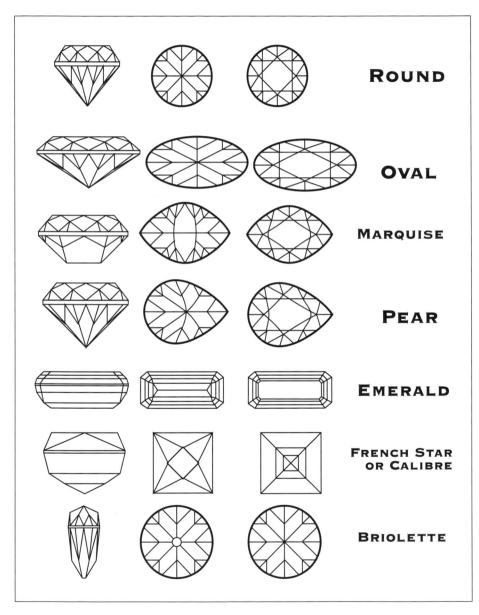

DIAGRAM F *A few of the hundreds of different faceting designs.*

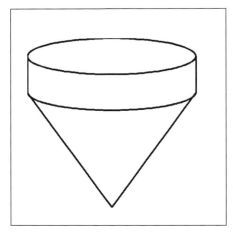

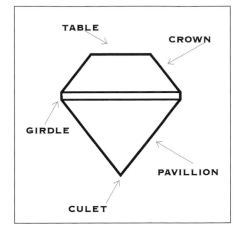

DIAGRAM G *Gemstone blank which has been ground to almost the exact shape in preparation for faceting.*

DIAGRAM H *The different parts of a faceted stone.*

After determining which design to use, the rough gemstone is trimmed and ground with a diamond impregnated saw and grinding wheel to a size as close to the final shape as possible (Diagram G). The effort expended to whittle down the stone as much as possible is immensely rewarded with time saved during subsequent procedures (Diagram H).

Since exact angles are needed to produce the precise mathematical size and location of each facet placed on the stone, the dop stick, with attached gem, cannot be held by hand, but, instead, must be securely positioned in a stable holding device known as a faceting head (see Photo 83). The faceting head has knobs and gears, all precisely indexed and labeled, which allow it to be moved to exact positions, determined by formulas and/or tables supplied in the books mentioned above. Those precise settings allow the gemstone to be ground to exactly the proper measurement when pressed against the spinning diamond impregnated lap at the base of the faceting machine.

Upon completing the first facet, all settings on the faceting head are changed according to formula, and the next one is placed on the stone, with the process continuing until the job is complete. Generally, opposite faces are done, one after the other, in order to preserve symmetry.

The procedure is then repeated with a finer grade abrasive, facet by facet, and then it is time to polish. The polish most universally used is tin oxide, but there are others. The polish paste is placed on the flat polishing wheel, and each facet is redone with the exact mathematical facet settings as before. Each facet is firmly pressed onto the polishing pad until flawless. Extreme patience and care are necessary when faceting since it is very easy to chip a corner off the stone, no matter how hard it might be.

□ CARVING

Carving, like faceting, takes considerably more skill, artistic ability, and patience than most other lapidary projects. There are many different types of tools available to carvers, the most popular of which are motorized, hand-held, flexible shaft, instruments, similar to those used by a dentist (Photo 85). Others are stationary, looking more like horizontal drill presses. The flexible shaft varieties are usually applied to the stone being carved. With the stationary types, the stone being carved is applied to the tool. Diamond impregnated carving points can be purchased in all sizes, shapes, and degrees of abrasiveness. Some are needle sharp, while others look like blunt balls or saucers (Photo 86).

PHOTO 85 *A flexible shaft carving tool with a selection of diamond bits.*

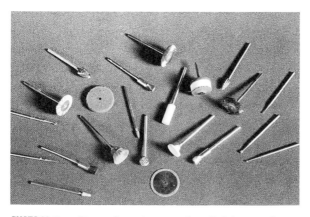

PHOTO 86 *Sanding, cleaning, and polishing tools for use on a motorized carving tool.*

Before the carving is started, it is necessary to make a sketch of the proposed object on all sides of the stone being shaped. Use a trim saw to remove absolutely as much excess material as possible. This can be done by making a series of adjacent saw cuts down to the edge of the outline and then breaking off what remains with a pair of pliers (Diagram I). Rough shaping with the carving tools is the most time consuming of all the steps and it seems to take forever to whittle down solid rock to a desired shape. Once shaped, detail can be added and progressive smoothing accomplished with tools of progressively finer and finer coarseness.

To polish the carving, it should first be thoroughly washed and then gently touched onto a

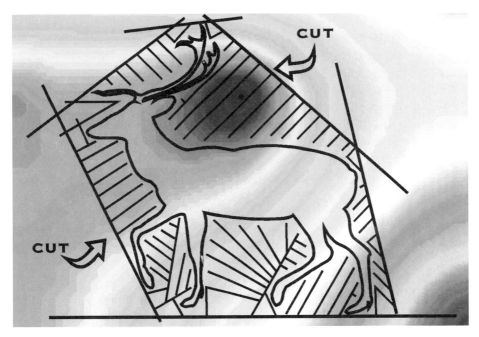

DIAGRAM I *A side view showing how to make parallel saw cuts into a block of stone being readied for carving.*

polishing wheel. As large a polishing wheel as possible should be used to get to the easily reached regions, but extreme care should be taken. The object should be kept cool and held tightly, since a motorized wheel can grab a sharp edge and send it flying with often disastrous consequences. The job is finished by using tiny polishing wheels attached to the powered carving tool in order to get into regions inaccessible by the large polishing wheel.

For intricate or fragile pieces, it is safest to polish the entire object with the tiny wheels in order to avoid breakage, even though it will take lots of time. Diamond polishing heads come in grits as fine as 14,000 and are as good or better than any powdered polish available.

CHAPTER 12 JEWELRY FROM GEMS & MINERALS

Colorful gemstones mounted in jewelry have been a measure of wealth and status in virtually every civilization dating back to the beginning of recorded history. In fact, even prehistorical graves reveal crude rings, bracelets, and hair decorations, buried with their owners. The Kings of ancient Mesopotamia, the Pharaohs of Egypt, the Emperors of China, and the great Maya, Inca, and Aztec rulers treasured their jewelry beyond all other possessions. There is something about a beautifully colored gemstone, with its clean transparency and often spectacular inner reflections of light that captivates the imagination and intensifies the desires of possession in humans.

In the past, only a few of the most skilled craftsmen had the technical knowledge and proficiency to make jewelry. They were highly respected amongst the powerful and wealthy, and what they fashioned was treasured. During the past century, however, the techniques for working with gemstones and precious metals have entered the domain of any person willing to take time to learn them. Equipment not available until relatively recent times, is now obtainable by anyone.

In fact, a person with absolutely no artistic talent can actually purchase pre-made settings for their stones. By doing a little gluing or bending of a few prongs, the amateur can produce results as nice as anything that can be purchased from a jeweler. Furthermore, there is a plethora of instruction manuals describing procedures for virtually any gem-cutting and jewelry-making technique imaginable. Most lapidary clubs and even many colleges offer enrichment courses in everything from silversmithing to gemstone appraisal. Just decide what you want to learn, and the possibilities for assistance are unlimited.

Surprisingly, the tools needed to make most types of jewelry are not overwhelmingly expensive and, in fact, you may have just about all you need for getting started in your own garage or workshop area. As you progress, however, you will certainly want to accumulate specialized items which can help increase quality and decrease frustration. The cost of making jewelry doesn't lie in equipment, but, instead in what types of metals and gemstones are used. Until you develop some skill, it is strongly suggested that you restrict your initial projects to relatively inexpensive but easy to work precious metals such as sterling silver and semiprecious stones like agate and jasper. Use something with which you can afford to make a few mistakes.

This chapter provides a brief look at how to make a few of the most basic types of jewelry. As was the case in Chapter 11, these are not thorough, step-by-step instructions covering every aspect or technique involved. If interest develops and you want to learn more, be sure to purchase a good book devoted to the specific topic of interest, subscribe to a jewelry-making magazine, and/or consider taking a class to help you along.

▫ THE STONES

Nice jewelry can be made from just about any small stones, ranging from little naturally-occurring crystals and chips, to very elaborately cut or carved polished gems. Before starting our first project, a few ideas are provided below, just to get you thinking.

Uncut or Unpolished Minerals

Beautiful pieces of jewelry can be made with unpolished, naturally occurring crystals or colorful mineral fragments. Such specimens can be mounted in necklaces, pins, bracelets or even rings, for a more natural look. If done tastefully, without the stone being too overbearing, the results can be very nice.

Tumbled Stones

Colorful tumbled agate, jasper, and other minerals can be utilized in many jewelry applications. There are limitless numbers of special holders and caps designed to attach tumbled stones to necklaces, bracelets, broaches, and even rings (Photo 87). Consider hanging some of your finest tumbled minerals on

PHOTO 87

Necklaces made with small tumbled stones.

a sterling silver or gold chain. If done with good taste, the resulting necklace can become a treasured piece of jewelry.

Cabochons

Cabochons are probably the most popular form of polished stones made by beginners and amateurs alike, and they can be used in just about any jewelry application which accommodates a flat backed stone such as rings, pendants, cuff links and bracelets. Most lapidary supply stores or catalogues sell pre-made settings made of everything from pot metal to sterling silver or gold to hold standard size cabochons (Photo 88.)

PHOTO 88 *Three cabochons, the one in the middle is used on a single stone necklace.*

Faceted Gems

Faceted gems generally find their place in rings or pendants. Pre-made settings can be purchased for faceted stones, just as was the case for cabochons, but not in such a huge range of sizes and shapes. For that reason, it is very important, if purchasing an already made setting, to be certain the stone is precisely the proper shape and size.

□ NECKLACES

Our first project involves stringing beads, which is one of the most ancient and enduring of all jewelry-making crafts. Necklaces can simply consist of a linked metal chain or inexpensive cord with a single stone attached at the apex, or they can be complex works of art with strands of beads made from just about anything from precious stones to plastic.

Beads can be purchased already drilled, sized, and ready to be strung at

134

most lapidary supply stores and bead shops. If, however, you choose to make a necklace from stones you have personally found and polished, be sure to read the discussion related to drilling in Chapter 11.

Tools

If you do want to try your hand at beading, a good pair of needle-nose pliers is handy for attaching clasps and jump rings, scissors are needed to cut the thread, and a ruler is helpful for measuring thread lengths and approximating bead size. In addition, a pair of tweezers is useful to assist with knot tying and picking up small beads, and transparent glue is good for securing clasps and preventing fraying on some types of thread.

In addition to the fundamental tools described above, it would be very helpful to purchase an inexpensive beading board, which is simply a tray composed of concentric grooves within which the beads can be placed and arranged to better layout the final design and symmetry of the necklace. In addition to a beading board, an awl or a beading needle will also help make things more enjoyable. A beading needle is the most versatile of the two, being made from flexible wire with a small twisted loop at the end, and it makes stringing beads a smooth operation. The thread is fed through the loop, and, as the loop enters the bead, it closes firmly, preventing the thread from slipping out.

Thread

A common error made by beginners is purchasing a thread that is either too thick to get through the smallest bead's hole or it is not strong enough to support everything. Try to use the thickest thread that will pass through all beads without fraying or separating.

Nylon is generally the best choice, since it doesn't fray or split like silk. It does tend to stretch, however, sometimes developing unsightly gaps between beads. If you learn to tie a knot between each bead, which is a good idea no matter which type thread you are using, the stretching problem will be minimized. Nylon thread can be purchased with a beading needle already attached, at predetermined lengths, in a variety of colors and thickness. Silk can also be purchased in a range of thicknesses and colors and is probably the easiest thread type to use when making knots between beads, since it is so smooth. When ordering thread, be sure it is at least 6 inches longer than you estimate will be needed to assure you have enough to accommodate the clasps and, if you choose, the knots.

Beads

When ordering or making beads to be used in a specific necklace, it is advisable to get a few more than you estimate will be needed. It never fails that one or two will be chipped or improperly drilled, and it is discouraging to stop everything and either order more or, worse yet, set up your shop and make more. When ordering beads, to help determine the approximate number you will need for a given length of necklace, the following table is provided. If you do not have the table handy and if all of your beads will be the same size (measured in millimeters), or you want a nonstandard length, use the following calculations to generate the number needed. (1) Multiply 25.4 by the length (in inches) which will provide the length in millimeters (since there are 25.4 millimeters in an inch). (2) Divide the number obtained in step 1 by the diameter (in millimeters) of the beads to be used. (3) The resulting number will be how many of that size of beads will be required to produce the desired length of necklace. Again, always add a few to the total to assure having enough.

Bead Size (mm)	~4"	16"	20"	24"	32"
3	34	136	170	204	271
4	26	102	127	153	204
5	21	82	102	123	163
6	17	68	85	102	136
7	15	59	74	88	117
8	13	51	64	77	102
10	11	41	51	61	82
12	9	34	43	51	68
14	8	30	37	44	59
16	7	26	32	39	51
18	6	23	29	34	46

Knots

The most fundamental type beading is accomplished by simply stringing thread through holes drilled in the stones or beads being used to make the necklace. The problem with such a simple procedure is that thread often stretches over time creating gaps, or, worse yet, if the thread should break, which does sometimes happen, there could be scores of beautiful beads and stones rolling everywhere.

To lessen the chances of such problems, and to also provide a slight buffer to deter the individual beads from directly hitting against each other, more advanced bead and necklace makers tie a knot on each bead, as briefly discussed earlier. That not only secures them in place but also minimizes disaster if the string should break. Knotting is not easy though, and requires lots of patience and practice.

To make a knot between each bead, start with a loose overhand knot and then, using an awl, tweezers, or beading needle, carefully slip it firmly against the bead while slowly tightening it. Practice is required in order to make sure the knot will not tighten completely before it is snugly in place. It is also important to be very careful not to allow the thread to tangle, twist, or self-knot. Always try to keep the thread straight and untwisted to alleviate tangling. If your knots tangle, self-knot, or tighten prematurely, it is usually difficult to untie them without damaging or weakening the thread, so be patient.

Procedure

The following six steps offer a fundamental summary for making a basic necklace. You will probably want to avoid knotting each bead in your first projects so other techniques can be learned. Eventually, however, if you pursue beading, the ability to knot the beads will be something you will want to learn. For more information on advanced stringing and knotting techniques, as mentioned many times before, consult a book exclusively dedicated to stringing beads.

(1) First, determine what type beads you want. Determine their size, shape, number required, etc. The beads can either be something you have made and drilled yourself, purchased at a lapidary supply store or bead shop, or ordered from catalogues.

(2) Procure the proper thickness, color, and type or thread desired, making sure it is at least 6" longer than your anticipated need.

(3) Tie a loose, but large knot at one end of the thread, which will serve as a stopper to prevent the beads from sliding off as you work.

(4) String the beads onto the thread to the desired length, cut off the excess thread, but be sure to leave enough for tying the ends together.

(5) Carefully untie the original knot and then tie the two loose ends together. Push the beads tight, equally on both sides of the just tied knot, and retie it as firmly as possible. This final knot is difficult to make, and should be as close to the end beads, on both sides, as possible. After you get this final knot tied, it is a good idea to double it, for security, one or two knots on top of each other.

(6) Cut the loose thread from the end and apply some transparent glue to the knot for additional security. The glue will not only prevent the ends from fraying, but it will also make it more permanent and less susceptible to untying.

Be sure to take plenty of time laying out your project so there is some sort of symmetry, especially if the beads have varying sizes and/or shapes, and then be especially careful that you string them in the correct order. This is especially true if you plan to knot between each bead. If you get just one out of order, it could require a complete restart, which can be discouraging.

□ RINGS, PENDANTS AND BRACELETS

Pre-Manufactured Settings

If you want to make jewelry such as rings, pendants, bracelets or other such items, the simplest way to accomplish that goal is to purchase ready-made mounts or findings at lapidary supply stores or though catalogues (Photo 89). They can be obtained in a range of qualities, intricacy, and, as you may have already guessed, price. The range of designs, sizes and shapes is almost limitless. Carefully cut your stone to a standard shape and size, as discussed in Chapter 11, place it into the pre-sized mounting, and secure it by bending the prongs around the stone.

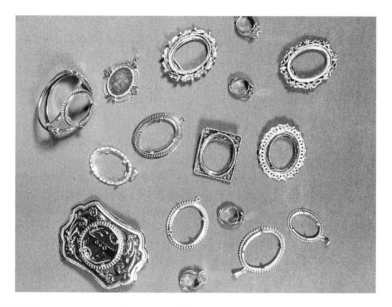

PHOTO 89 *A selection of sterling silver preforms upon which you can attach cabochons or, in the case of the rings, faceted stones.*

The entire process, if all sizing was done properly, will only take a few minutes, and the results can be extremely professional. The only tool you will need is a prong setter and/or bezel pusher, which can be purchased at most lapidary supply stores (Photo 90). The cost is only a few dollars, and such a tool allows you to accomplish the task far better than if you use a screwdriver or other such household tool.

If mounting a faceted stone, attempt to get each prong firmly attached directly to a flat facet surface. Start with one prong and gently bend it over the stone, then go to the opposite side and do another, then do one of the remaining prongs, etc. Most rings only have four stone setting prongs, but, occasionally, there are more.

After you have initially centered the stone and secured it with the prongs, go back and further tighten the first prong, then the second, etc., repeating the process until the gem is firmly and evenly set. Do not over tighten any prong prematurely, since that could force the stone out of proper alignment with the setting. You do not want to continually bend and unbend the prongs either, since they will quickly lose their holding power or can be broken off. Do the job slowly and carefully the first time.

PHOTO 90 *Two different types of bezel pushers (on each side) and a prong setter (in the middle).*

Basic Metalsmithing

If you want to try making your own mountings, and you are willing to spend some time practicing, the craft of silversmithing (or goldsmithing if you have plenty of money) is fun to learn and extremely satisfying. Be sure to get the proper equipment, which really doesn't cost very much and makes the job much easier. Scratches or flaws on the surface of a brightly polished metallic mounting caused by using makeshift tools can be unsightly and difficult if not impossible to remove.

What follows is a brief overview of the process used to make simple sterling silver mountings for cabochons. The mounting being described could be used on a ring, bracelet, or pendant.

(1) Make a sketch of what you want the base to look like, keeping in mind that it should be larger than the cabochon to be mounted upon it. When you are satisfied with your creation, redraw it onto a sheet of sterling silver (Diagram J), which can be purchased at most lapidary stores, in a range of thicknesses.

It is suggested that you start with material that is not too thin, and advice can be obtained from your supplier.

(2) The cabochon is then placed onto the silver sheet, exactly where it should be within the confines of the earlier sketched base, and a pencil or scribe is used to mark precisely around its circumference.

139

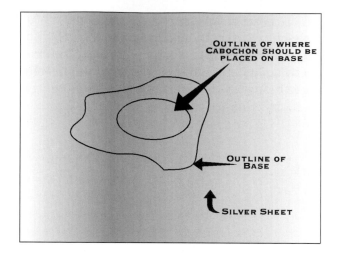

DIAGRAM J *The outline of the base of a proposed silversmithing project.*

(3) Next, roughly trim the sheet with a pair of small tin snips (Diagram K) and then follow the outline with a jewelers saw (Diagram L), being careful to stay just outside the proposed outline. Touch things up by using a small file to smooth the outline of the base to exactly the desired size.

(4) Step 4 involves making the all important bezel (Diagram M). Special bezel metal, generally a thin strip of more pure silver, can be purchased at any lapidary supply store. In order to cut the bezel metal to the proper length, a thin length of wire is wrapped around the base of the cabochon to be mounted and the ends tightly twisted. The wire is then cut in the middle, straightened out, and the resulting length will precisely measure the circumference of the stone to be mounted.

DIAGRAM K *Using tin snips to cut around the proposed base for a silversmithing project.*

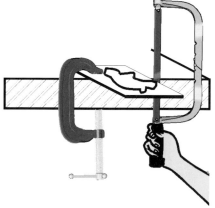

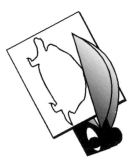

DIAGRAM L *Carefully cutting just outside the border of the base for the proposed silversmithing project with a jewelers saw.*

(5) A a strip of the bezel metal is stretched out next to the wire described in step 4, and carefully cut to exactly the same length.

DIAGRAM M *A typical bezel.*

(6) The properly sized bezel should be gently curled by running it through the fingers so it makes a loop with each end touching. It is then soldered together using silver solder and a small hand-held propane torch, on a charcoal block.

Silver solder comes in sheets, categorized as hard, medium or soft, depending upon the melting temperature. Little squares (called snippets), measuring about one-eighth of an inch on a side, are then cut from the sheet with small tin snips (Photo 91).

PHOTO 91 *Making snippets of silver solder.*

The process of silver soldering involves first brushing flux on all areas to be joined, in order to remove oxidation, and then laying an appropriate number of silver solder snippets onto the joint. The torch is moved continuously near the joint but not directly on it. Bezels are easily melted, so the torch must be kept moving. When things get sufficiently hot, the solder will melt and flow into the joint.

(7) Once the solder flows, remove the torch and allow it to harden. Take the bezel from the charcoal block with copper or wooden tongs and dip into a pickling solution to remove any black oxidation caused by the heating. After pickling, the bezel should be carefully rinsed and allowed to dry.

(8) The bezel loop is then placed over the base of the cabochon to be mounted and rubbed so that it will retain the shape. This step of "working the bezel" to the exact shape of the cabochon is extremely important, and if not done properly, the entire project could be in trouble.

(9) Next, the "molded" bezel is gently placed onto the silver base which was prepared in Steps 1, 2 and 3, making sure it is exactly on the earlier drawn outline of the cabochon. The edge of the bezel should lay perfectly flat onto the base and adjustments should be made if that is not the case.

(10) Flux should be brushed onto the bottom edge of the bezel and the base, at the point where the bezel is to be soldered. Snippets of solder are leaned onto the bezel about every one-eighth of an inch or so all the way around (Diagram N).

(11) The torch is first applied to the bezel, as before, and, once heated, the flame is directed toward the base, again, continu-

DIAGRAM N *The bezel on the silver sheet in place to be soldered.*

ally moving it all around near where the bezel makes contact. Continue this process as the metal becomes progressively hotter and hotter until the solder is sucked into the joint, completely around the bottom of the bezel.

(12) After the soldering is complete, use your tongs to dip it into the warm pickling solution and then rinse and carefully dry it.

DROPS   **TWISTED WIRE AROUND BEZEL**

DIAGRAM O *A few different types of ornamentation which can be placed around the bezel.*

(13) Additional decoration and embellishment, and/or the ring shank or pin back, etc. can now be soldered to the base in the same way the bezel was attached (Diagram O).

(14) Smooth all edges with a fine jeweler's file. Then the silver can be polished, either with an electric buffer, or by hand. A hand held, flexible shaft tool, as discussed in Chapter 11, works very well for polishing silver, and polishing pads of all shapes can be purchased for such tools. A final polish can be applied by hand with jewelers rouge or a coated polishing cloth.

(15) When all metalwork is completed, the stone should be placed inside the bezel, and the bezel tightened around the stone (Diagram P & Q). Tightening a bezel is similar to settings prongs. Use a bezel pusher tool and do a little at a time, working around the stone many times until the bezel is snug around the base of the cabochon.

DIAGRAM P *A stone set in a plain bezel.*

142

As was the case with prong settings, if you must reopen a bezel due to an uneven mounting, it is very difficult to re-tighten it without unsightly bend marks.

DIAGRAM Q *Tightening a bezel around a cabochon using a bezel-pushing tool.*

Lost Wax

Another way to make gemstone mountings is to use the lost wax technique. Most commercial ring mountings are not made by the silver soldering process just described, but, instead, are produced by the lost wax molding process. Briefly, this is a process which starts with a wax model of the desired shape and size which is either hand carved or purchased from a lapidary supply source.

The wax model is encased in what is called an investment, which is something like plaster of Paris. Before the investment completely dries around the mold, one or a few holes, called sprue holes, are carefully bored through the plaster to the surface of the encased wax mold.

After the investment is completely dry and hardened, it is placed inside a kiln and heated to a temperature of over 1,000 degrees farenheit. The heat causes the wax to not only melt but actually vaporize, with the vapors escaping through the sprue holes, leaving a perfect void inside the investment, with its outer surface an exact replica of the original wax mold. The vaporization of the wax and its "disappearance" from the investment is where the term lost wax process originates.

Once the wax has been completely vaporized out of the investment, molten metal, usually sterling silver or gold, is poured into one or more of the sprue holes to refill the cavity. The metal is allowed to cool, the investment is cracked open, and the inside will be an exact replica, in precious metal, of the original wax mold. The casting is buffed, smoothed and then polished.

Lost wax casting requires some special equipment and lots of artistic skill if you plan to design your own molds. This is a more advanced process, but certainly worth considering if you want to invest some money and time into learning how to do it. It takes lots of practice to get things just right. The problem most people have with the lost wax process is the formation of bubbles within the metal, especially on the surface, which are sometimes impossible to buff out. Making a good, smooth-surfaced casting requires time, patience, and practice.

SUGGESTED SPECIMEN LABELS

APPENDIX A

QUARTZ CRYSTAL

QUARTZ CRYSTAL

Crystal Hill, Arizona

QUARTZ CRYSTAL
Crystal Hill, Arizona

#214   2/23/87

QUARTZ CRYSTAL
Crystal Hill, Arizona

#214   2/23/87
J. R. Mitchell
Photo #1217-1220

COLLECTION OF JAMES R. MITCHELL

Species: Quartz   Specimen Number: 214
Type: Crystal   Size: 1-1/2 " x 2-3/4" x 4-1/2"

Location: Crystal Hill, Arizona
Notes: Found facing west, about half way to the top, in a cavity
Purchased from: Rick Eveleth   Date: 2/13/87   Cost: $12.00

COLLECTION OF JAMES R. MITCHELL

Species: Quartz   Specimen Number: 214
Type: Crystal   Size: 1-1/2 " x 2-3/4" x 4-1/2"

Location: Crystal Hill, Arizona
Notes: Found facing west, about half way to the top, in a cavity
Collected By: James R. Mitchell   Date: 2/13/87   Value: $12.00

APPENDIX B COMMONLY ENCOUNTERED MINERALS

Appendix B consists of seven tables, each providing an arrangement of the minerals described in Chapter 5, sorted by different properties. For similar information related to additional minerals, extensive tables are provided in just about any good mineral identification book. Appendix B and Chapter 5, however, will help you get started.

If you are in a region known to produce one or more of the minerals described in Chapter 5, these tables should be supportive in at least sorting them out. To use them, conduct as many of the tests and observations as you can, continually narrowing down the possibilities. When you think you have made a positive identification, read the detailed descriptions related to the particular mineral in Chapter 5 to confirm your selection.

For example: If you are in an area known to produce barite and your mineral in question is colorless, can easily be scratched with a knife blade, has a white streak, and has tabular crystals, you can eliminate most other possibilities in regard to the Chapter 5 minerals. Obviously, it still could be something else, but, knowing in advance that barite is found in collectable quantities at that location, certainly serves to support your choice. In fact, one of the prime aids in mineral identification is doing research related to the mineralization at the locality where the mineral in question was found. Field trip guidebooks are very helpful in that regard.

COMMONLY ENCOUNTERED MINERALS BY COLOR

Color	Mineral	Hardness	Specific Gravity	Color of Streak	Luster	Crystal System	Fracture Type
Amber	Mica	2.5 - 3.0	2.8	Colorless	Glassy - Pearly	Monoclinic	Uneven
Any Color (light)	Opal	5.5 - 6.5	2	White	Glassy - Pearly	None	Conchoidal
Black	Azurite	3.5 - 4.0	3.8	Blue (light)	Dull	Monoclinic	Conchoidal
Black	Corundum	9.0	4	White	Glassy	Hexagonal	Conchoidal
Black	Feldspar	6.0 - 6.5	2.5 - 2.7	White	Glassy - Pearly	Mono- or Triclinic	Uneven
Black	Fluorite	4.0	3.1	White	Glassy	Isometric	Uneven or Conchoidal
Black	Garnet	6.5 - 7.5	3.5 - 4.3	White	Glassy	Isometric	Conchoidal
Black	Hematite	5.0 - 6.0	4.9 - 5.3	Red	Metallic	Hexagonal	Uneven or Splintery
Black	Mica	2.5 - 3.0	2.8	Colorless	Glassy - Pearly	Monoclinic	Uneven
Black	Serpentine	3.0 - 5.0	2.3 - 2.6	White (usually)	Waxy - Silky	None	Splintery or Conchoidal
Black	Tourmaline	7.0 - 7.5	3.0 - 3.3	White	Glassy	Hexagonal	Uneven or Conchoidal
Black (smoky)	Quartz	7.0	2.65	White	Glassy	Hexagonal	Conchoidal
Black (tarnish)	Silver	2.5 - 3.0	10.1 - 11.1	White (silvery)	Metallic	Isometric (rare)	Hackly
Blue	Azurite	3.5 - 4.0	3.8	Blue (light)	Dull	Monoclinic	Conchoidal
Blue	Beryl	7.5 - 8.0	2.6 - 2.9	White/colorless	Glassy	Hexagonal	Conchoidal or Uneven
Blue	Chalcedony	7.0	2.6	White	Waxy - Glassy	None	Conchoidal
Blue	Corundum	9.0	4	White	Glassy	Hexagonal	Conchoidal
Blue	Feldspar	6.0 - 6.5	2.5 - 2.7	White	Glassy - Pearly	Mono- or Triclinic	Uneven

COMMONLY ENCOUNTERED MINERALS BY COLOR

Color	Mineral	Hardness	Specific Gravity	Color of Streak	Luster	Crystal System	Fracture Type
Blue	Fluorite	4.0	3.1	White	Glassy	Isometric	Uneven or Conchoidal
Blue	Tourmaline	7.0 - 7.5	3.0 - 3.3	White	Glassy	Hexagonal	Conchoidal or Uneven
Blue (light)	Barite	3.0 - 3.5	4.4	White	Glassy - Pearly	Orthorhombic	Uneven
Blue (sky blue)	Chrysocolla	2.0 - 4.0	2.0 - 2.3	White	Glassy - Waxy	Monoclinic	Conchoidal
Bluish (Light)	Halite	2.0 - 2.5	2.16	White	Glassy	Isometric	Conchoidal
Brass Yellow	Pyrite	6.0 - 6.5	4.9 - 5.2	Brownish black	Metallic	Isometric	Uneven
Bronze	Bornite	3.0	5.0	Grayish black	Metallic	Isometric (rare)	Uneven or Conchoidal
Brown	Barite	3.0 - 3.5	4.4	White	Glassy - Pearly	Orthorhombic	Uneven
Brown	Chalcedony	7.0	2.6	White	Waxy - Glassy	None	Conchoidal
Brown	Corundum	9.0	4	White	Glassy	Hexagonal	Conchoidal
Brown	Feldspar	6.0 - 6.5	2.5 - 2.7	White	Glassy - Pearly	Mono- or Triclinic	Uneven
Brown	Fluorite	4.0	3.1	White	Glassy	Isometric	Conchoidal
Brown	Garnet	6.5 - 7.5	3.5 - 4.3	White	Glassy	Isometric	Conchoidal
Brown	Quartz	7.0	2.65	White	Glassy	Hexagonal	Conchoidal
Brown	Serpentine	3.0 - 5.0	2.3 - 2.6	White (usually)	Waxy - Silky	None	Splintery or Conchoidal
Brown	Tourmaline	7.0 - 7.5	3.0 - 3.3	White	Glassy	Hexagonal	Uneven or Conchoidal
Brownish Black	Mica	2.5 - 3.0	2.8	Colorless	Glassy - Pearly	Monoclinic	Uneven
Brownish Red	Garnet	6.5 - 7.5	3.5 - 4.4	White	Glassy	Isometric	Conchoidal

COMMONLY ENCOUNTERED MINERALS BY COLOR

Color	Mineral	Hardness	Specific Gravity	Color of Streak	Luster	Crystal System	Fracture Type
Colorless	Barite	3.0 - 3.5	4.4	White	Glassy - Pearly	Orthorhombic	Uneven
Colorless	Calcite	3.0	2.7	White	Glassy	Hexagonal	Conchoidal
Colorless	Chalcedony	7.0	2.6	White	Waxy - Glassy	None	Conchoidal
Colorless	Corundum	9.0	4	White	Glassy	Hexagonal	Conchoidal
Colorless	Fluorite	4.0	3.1	White	Glassy	Isometric	Conchoidal or Uneven
Colorless	Gypsum	1.5 - 2.0	2.3	White	Glassy - Pearly	Monoclinic	Conchoidal or Splintery
Colorless	Halite	2.0 - 2.5	2.16	White	Glassy	Isometric	Conchoidal
Colorless	Mica	2.5 - 3.0	2.8	Colorless	Glassy - Pearly	Monoclinic	Uneven
Colorless	Opal	5.5 - 6.5	2	White	Glassy - Pearly	None	Conchoidal
Colorless	Quartz	7.0	2.65	White	Glassy	Hexagonal	Conchoidal
Gold	Chalcedony	7.0	2.6	White	Waxy - Glassy	None	Conchoidal
Gold	Gold	2.5 - 3.0	15.6 - 19.3	Golden yellow	Metallic	Isometric	Hackly
Gray (lead gray)	Galena	2.5 - 2.7	7.4 - 7.6	Gray (lead gray)	Metallic	Isometric	Slight Conchoidal
Gray (steel)	Hematite	5.0 - 6.0	4.9 - 5.3	Red	Metallic	Hexagonal	Uneven - Splintery
Green	Beryl	7.5 - 8.0	2.7	White / colorless	Glassy	Hexagonal	Conchoidal or Uneven
Green	Chrysocolla	2.0 - 4.0	2.0 - 2.3	White	Glassy - Waxy	Monoclinic	Conchoidal
Green	Feldspar	6.0 - 6.5	2.5 - 2.7	White	Glassy - Pearly	Mono- or Triclinic	Uneven

COMMONLY ENCOUNTERED MINERALS BY COLOR

Color	Mineral	Hardness	Specific Gravity	Color of Streak	Luster	Crystal System	Fracture Type
Green	Fluorite	4.0	3.1	White	Glassy	Isometric	Conchoidal or Uneven
Green	Garnet	6.5 - 7.5	3.5 - 4.4	White	Glassy	Isometric	Conchoidal
Green	Malachite	3.5 - 4.0	3.9	Light Green	Silky, Dull	Monoclinic	Splintery or Conchoidal
Green	Mica	2.5 - 3.0	2.8	Colorless	Glassy - Pearly	Monoclinic	Uneven
Green	Serpentine	3.0 - 5.0	2.3 - 2.6	White (usually)	Waxy - Silky	None	Splintery or Conchoidal
Green	Tourmaline	7.0 - 7.5	3.0 - 3.3	White	Glassy	Hexagonal	Uneven or Conchoidal
Greenish Black	Mica	2.5 - 3.0	2.8	Colorless	Glassy - Pearly	Monoclinic	Uneven
Greenish Blue	Chrysocolla	2.0 - 4.0	2.0 - 2.3	White	Glassy - Waxy	Monoclinic	Conchoidal
Light Tints	Gypsum	1.5 - 2.0	2.3	White	Glassy - Pearly	Monoclinic	Conchoidal or Splintery
Multi-Hued	Tourmaline	7.0 - 7.5	3.0 - 3.3	White	Glassy	Hexagonal	Uneven or Conchoidal
Orange	Garnet	6.5 - 7.5	3.5 - 4.3	White	Glassy	Isometric	Conchoidal
Pale Hues	Calcite	3.0	2.7	White	Glassy	Hexagonal	Conchoidal
Pink	Beryl	7.5 - 8.0	2.7	White / colorless	Glassy	Hexagonal	Conchoidal or Uneven
Pink	Chalcedony	7.0	2.6	White	Waxy - Glassy	None	Conchoidal
Pink	Garnet	6.5 - 7.5	3.5 - 4.3	White	Glassy	Isometric	Conchoidal
Pink	Quartz	7.0	2.65	White	Glassy	Hexagonal	Conchoidal

COMMONLY ENCOUNTERED MINERALS BY COLOR

Color	Mineral	Hardness	Specific Gravity	Color of Streak	Luster	Crystal System	Fracture Type
Pink	Tourmaline	7.0 - 7.5	3.0 - 3.3	White	Glassy	Hexagonal	Unven or Conchoidal
Purple (deep)	Garnet	6.5 - 7.5	3.5 - 4.3	White	Glassy	Isometric	Conchoidal
Purplish Red	Garnet	6.5 - 7.5	3.5 - 4.3	White	Glassy	Isometric	Conchoidal
Red	Chalcedony	7.0	2.6	White	Waxy - Glassy	None	Conchoidal
Red	Corundum	9.0	4.0	White	Glassy	Hexagonal	Conchoidal
Red	Hematite	5.0 - 6.0	4.9 - 5.35	Red	Metallic	Hexagonal	Uneven - Splintery
Red	Serpentine	3.0 - 5.0	2.3 - 2.6	White (usually)	Waxy - Silky	None	Splintery or Conchoidal
Red	Tourmaline	7.0 - 7.5	3.0 - 3.3	White	Glassy	Hexagonal	Uneven or Conchoidal
Reddish	Feldspar	6.0 - 6.5	2.5 - 2.7	White	Glassy - Pearly	Mono- or Triclinic	Uneven
Reddish (light)	Halite	2.0 - 2.5	2.16	White	Glassy	Isometric	Conchoidal
Reddish Brown	Barite	3.0 - 3.5	4.4	White	Glassy - Pearly	Orthorhombic	Uneven
Reddish Brown	Feldspar	6.0 - 6.5	2.5 - 2.7	White	Glassy - Pearly	Mono- or Triclinic	Uneven
Rose	Mica	2.5 - 3.0	2.8	Colorless	Glassy - Pearly	Monoclinic	Uneven
Silver	Hematite	5.0 - 6.0	4.9 - 5.3	Red	Metallic	Hexagonal	Uneven - Splintery
Silver White	Silver	2.5 - 3.0	10.1 - 11.1	White (silvery)	Metallic	Isometric (rare)	Hackly
Silvery Yellow	Gold	2.5 - 3.0	15.6- 19.3	Golden Yellow	Metallic	Isometric	Hackly
Tarnished	Bornite	3.0	5.0	Grayish Black	Metallic	Isometric (rare)	Uneven
Violet	Corundum	9.0	4.0	White	Glassy	Hexagonal	Conchoidal

COMMONLY ENCOUNTERED MINERALS BY COLOR

Color	Mineral	Hardness	Specific Gravity	Color of Streak	Luster	Crystal System	Fracture Type
Violet	Fluorite	4.0	3.1	White	Glassy	Isometric	Uneven or Conchoidal
Violet	Quartz	7.0	2.65	White	Glassy	Hexagonal	Conchoidal
Violet Red (deep)	Garnet	6.5 - 7.5	3.5 - 4.3	White	Glassy	Isometric	Conchoidal
White	Beryl	7.5 - 8.0	2.7	White or Colorless	Glassy	Hexagonal	Uneven or Conchoidal
White	Calcite	3.0	2.7	White	Glassy	Hexagonal	Conchoidal
White	Chalcedony	7.0	2.6	White	Waxy - Glassy	None	Conchoidal
White	Feldspar	6.0 - 6.5	2.5 - 2.7	White	Glassy - Pearly	Mono- or Triclinic	Uneven
White	Fluorite	4.0	3.1	White	Glassy	Isometric	Uneven or Conchoidal
White	Gypsum	1.5 - 2.0	2.3	White	Glassy - Pearly	Monoclinic	Conchoidal or Splintery
White	Halite	2.0 - 2.5	2.16	White	Glassy	Isometric	Conchoidal
White	Mica	2.5 - 3.0	2.8	Colorless	Glassy - Pearly	Monoclinic	Uneven
White	Quartz	7.0	2.65	White	Glassy	Hexagonal	Conchoidal
White	Serpentine	3.0 -5.0	2.3 - 2.6	White (usually)	Waxy - Silky	None	Splintery or Conchoidal
White	Tourmaline	7.0 - 7.5	3.0 - 3.3	White	Glassy	Hexagonal	Uneven or Conchoidal
Yellow	Beryl	7.5 - 8.0	2.7	White or Colorless	Glassy	Hexagonal	Uneven or Conchoidal
Yellow	Chalcedony	7.0	2.6	White	Waxy - Glassy	None	Conchoidal

COMMONLY ENCOUNTERED MINERALS BY COLOR

Color	Mineral	Hardness	Specific Gravity	Color of Streak	Luster	Crystal System	Fracture Type
Yellow	Corundum	9.0	4.0	White	Glassy	Hexagonal	Conchoidal
Yellow	Feldspar	6.0 - 6.5	2.5 - 2.7	White	Glassy - Pearly	Mono- or triclinic	Uneven
Yellow	Fluorite	4.0	3.1	White	Glassy	Isometric	Conchoidal or Uneven
Yellow	Gold	3.0	19.3	Golden yellow	Metallic	Isometric	Hackly
Yellow	Mica	2.5 - 3.0	2.8	Colorless	Glassy - Pearly	Monoclinic	Uneven
Yellow	Serpentine	3.0 - 5.0	2.3 - 2.6	White (usually)	Waxy - Silky	None	Splintery or Conchoidal
Yellow (light)	Barite	3.0 - 3.5	4.4	White	Glassy - Pearly	Orthorhombic	Uneven

APPENDIX C GOVERNMENT AGENCIES

U.S. Bureau of Land Management
Office of Public Affairs
1849 C St., Room 406-LS
Washington, D.C. 20240
(202)452-5125

U.S.D.A. Forest Service
P.O. Box 96090
Washington, D.C. 20090
(202) 205-8333

U.S. Department of Interior
U.S. Geological Survey-Minerals Info.
988 National Center
Reston, VA 20192
http://minerals.usgs.gov/minerals

USGS Information Services
Box 25268
Denver, CO 80225
http://mapping.usgs.gov/esic/
to_order.html

Geological Survey of Alabama
Univ. of Alabama, P.O. Drawer O
University, AL 35486-9780
(205) 349-2852

Alaska Geological Survey
794 University Avenue, Suite 200
Fairbanks, AK 99709-3645
(907) 451-5000

Arizona Geological Survey
416 W. Congress St., Suite 100
Tucson, AZ 85701
(520) 770-3500

Arkansas Geological Commission
3815 West Roosevelt Road
Little Rock, AR 72204
(501) 663-3760

California Geological Survey
801 K Street, MS 12-30
Sacramento, CA 95814-3531
(916) 445-1825

Colorado Geological Survey
Bldg. 53, Denver Federal Center
Mailstop 425, Box 25046
Lakewood, CO 80225
(303) 866-2611

Connecticut Geological Survey
Natural Resources Center
79 Elm Street
Hartford, CT 06106
(860) 424-3540

Delaware Geological Survey
University of Delaware
Newark, DE 19716-7501
(302)831-2833

Florida Geological Survey
903 West Tennessee Street
Gunter Building MS #720
Tallahassee, FL 32304-7700
(850) 488-4191

Georgia Dept. of Natural Resources
19 Martin Luther King Jr. Drive, S.W.
Fourth Floor, Agriculture Building
Atlanta, GA 30334

Hawaii USGS State Representative
677 Ala Moana Blvd.
Honolulu, HI 96813
(808) 587-2400

Idaho Geological Survey
University of Idaho
Room 332, Morrill Hall
Moscow, ID 83843
(208) 855-7991

Illinois Geological Survey
Natural Resources Building
615 Peabody Drive
Champaign, IL 61820-6964
(217) 333-4747

Indiana Geological Survey
Indiana University
611 N. Walnut Grove
Bloomington, IN 47405-2222
(812) 855-7636

Iowa Geological Survey
Indiana Univ., 109 Trowbridge Hall
Iowa City, IA 52242-1319
(319) 335-1575

Kansas Geological Survey
1930 Constant Avenue
West Campus, Univ. of Kansas
Lawrence, KS 66047
(785) 864-3965

Kentucky Geological Survey
228 Mining & Mineral Resources Bldg.
Room 104, University of Kentucky
Lexington, KY 40506-0107
(859) 257-5500

Louisiana Geological Survey
LSU, P.O. Box G
Baton Rouge, LA 70893
(504) 388-5320

Maine Geological Survey
Department of Conservation
22 State House Station
Augusta, ME 04333-0022
(207) 287-2801

Maryland Geological Survey
2300 St. Paul Street
Baltimore, MD 21218-5210
(410) 554-5500

Massachusetts Geological Survey
233 Morrill Science Center
Univ. of MA, 611 N. Pleasant St.
Amherst, MA 01003-9297
(413) 545-2286

Michigan Geological Survey
Geologic & Land Management Div.
P.O. Box 30258
Lansing, MI 48909-7756
(515) 334-6907

Minnesota Geological Survey
University of Minnesota
2642 University Avenue
St. Paul, MN 55114-1057
(612) 627-4780

Mississippi Office of Geology
P.O. Box 20307
Jackson, MS 39289-1307
(601) 961-5500

Missouri Geological Survey
Department of Natural Resources
P.O. Box 250
Rolla, MO 65401-0250
(537) 368-2100

Montana Bureau of Mines & Geology
Federal Building , Room 428
1300 West Park Street
Butte, MT 59701-8997
(406) 496-4180

Nebraska Conservation and Survey
  Division, University of Nebraska
113 Nebraska Hall
Lincoln, NE 68588-0517
(402) 472-3471

Nevada Bureau of Mines & Geology
University of Nevada, Reno, MS 178
Reno, NV 89557-0088
(775) 784-6691

New Hampshire Geological Survey
Dept. of Environmental Services
6 Hazen Drive, Box 95
Concord, NH 03302-0095
(603) 271-6428

New Jersey Geological Survey
Dept. of Environmental Protection
29 Arctic Parkway, P. O. Box CN-427
Trenton, NJ 08625
(609) 292-1185

New Mexico Bureau of Mines
  and Mineral Resources
Campus Station, New Mexico Tech.
Socorro, New Mexico 87801
(505) 835-5420

New York Academy of Minerology
Empire State Plaza
3140 Cultural Education Center
Albany, NY 12230
(518) 474-5816

North Carolina Geological Survey
Division of Land Resources
1612 Mail Service Center
Raleigh, NC 27699-1612
(919) 733-2423

North Dakota Geological Survey
600 East Boulevard
Bismark, ND 58505-0840
(701) 328-8000

Ohio Geological Survey
Div. of Natural Resources
4383 Fountain Square Drive
Columbus, OH 43224
(614) 265-6576

Oklahoma Geological Survey
Univeristy of Oklahoma
100 East Boyd, Room N-131
Norman, OK 73019-0628
(405) 325-3031

Oregon Department of Geology
  and Mineral Industries
800 N.E. Oregon Street, Suite 965
Portland, OR 97232
(503) 731-4100

Pennsylvania Geological Survey
Department of Natural Resources
3240 Schoolhouse Rd.
Middleton, PA 17057
(717) 702-2017

Office of Rhode Island State Geologist
Department of Geology
315 Green Hall
University of Rhode Island
Kingston, RI 02881
(401) 874-2265

South Carolina Geological Survey
5 Geology Road
Stephenson Center, Suite 129
Columbia, SC 29212
(803) 896-7700

South Dakota Dept. of Environment
    and Natural Resources
Univ. of SD, Science Center
Vermillion, SD 57069-2390
(605) 677-5227

Tennessee Division of Geology
401 Church Street
Nashville, TN 37243-0445
(615) 532-1500

Texas Bureau of Economic Geology
The University of Texas at Austin
Box X, University Station
Austin, TX 78713-8924
(512) 471-1534

Utah Geological Survey
1594 W. North Temple
P.O. Box 146100
Salt Lake City, UT 84114-6100
(801) 537-3300

Vermont Geological Survey
Agency of Natural Resources
103 South Main, Landry Building
Waterbury, VT 05671-0301
(802) 241-3608

Virginia Div. of Mineral Resources
Box 3667
Charlottesville, VA 22903
(804) 293-5121

Washington Division of Geology
    and Earth Resources
1111 Washington St. SE, Room 148
Olympia, WA 98501
(360) 902-1450

West Virginia Geological Survey
P.O. Box 879
Morgantown, WV 26507-0879
(304) 594-2331

Wisconsin Geological Survey
University of Wisconsin
3817 Mineral Point Road
Madison, WI 53705-5100
(608) 262-8086

Wyoming State Geological Survey
Box 3008
University Station
Laramie, WY 82071-3008
(307) 766-2286

APPENDIX D

GLOSSARY OF USEFUL TERMS

Abrasives: These are the materials used to shape and smooth gemstones. Abrasives are often referred to as grits, and come in different degrees of coarseness. When working on rock, lapidaries start with the most coarse, for rough shaping, and then gradually use finer and finer grades to prepare the stone for polishing. Generally, lapidary abrasives are made from silicon carbide.

Acetylene Torch: A type of torch often used by advanced silversmiths.

Adamantine: A luster that is extremely bright, like a diamond.

Adularescence: A special effect exhibited in some minerals where a milky, cloud-like reflection of light seems to billow within the polished stone. Moonstone, with its silvery, floating "cloud," is a good example.

Agatized: Any prehistoric organic object, such as bone or wood, that maintains its original structure, but has been completely replaced by agate. A good example is agatized wood.

Alcohol Lamp: A glass lamp with a wick which uses alcohol as fuel. Alcohol lamps are used primarily for low heat lapidary work such as melting wax for dopping stones.

Alluvial: A concentration of minerals or other material formed by erosion.

Aluminum Pencil: A pencil-shaped aluminum marker used to draw outlines of shapes onto stone. The aluminum mark will not wash off with water, making it very useful for lapidary applications.

Amorphous: Does not have a crystal structure.

Amygdule: A void within a volcanic rock that was formed by a gas bubble. Amygdules sometimes contain other minerals such as calcite and quartz.

Apex: In a faceted stone, the apex is the bottom most point.

Arroyo: A wash.

Asterism: A star-like effect exhibited by some polished stones.

Axis: An imaginary line around which the symmetry of a crystal is oriented.

Bar: A deposit of sand or gravel within a river or stream.

Basalt: A common, dark, igneous rock.

Bead Board: A grooved board used to arrange beads for use in a necklace, before stringing.

Bead Thread: Thread, usually made from either silk or nylon, used for stringing beads.

Bedding: The layering effect of sedimentary rocks.

Bedrock: The solid rock that lies under the loose sand or other soils.

Bell Cap: A bell-shaped cap used to attach polished stones (usually tumbled) to lapidary objects such as necklaces or pendants.

Bezel: A thin, flat band of soft metal used in jewelry to hold a stone in place.

Bezel Pusher: A jeweler's tool used to bend and smooth a bezel around stones being set in jewelry.

Bladed: A flat, thin, blade-shaped crystallization such as demonstrated by some occurrences of barite.

Botryoidal: A massive mineral occurrence which looks like bubbles or grapes, as often exhibited by chalcedony and malachite.

Breccia: A rock composed of angular fragments cemented together. Regions between the fragments are often hollow and contain tiny crystals.

Buff: A polishing pad customarily made from felt or leather.

Cabbing: The act of cutting and polishing a cabochon.

Cabochon: A polished stone with a flat bottom and smooth domed top, either round, oval, square or rectangular in shape.

Carat: The unit used to express the weight of gemstones. A carat is about one-one hundred fiftieth of an ounce and it takes 5 carats to equal one gram.

Carborundum: A very hard, synthetic material made from silicon carbide used to make grinding wheels, tumbling and sanding grits, and other lapidary tools.

Casting: In jewelry, casting involves the injection of molten metal into a mold, allowing it to cool, then breaking it open to provide a metal object with shape fixed by the mold.

Casting Machine: A machine made to simplify the process of metal casting.

Casting Wax: The material most often used to make the mold for casting settings to be used for jewelry.

Cat's Eye: A phenomenon exhibited by some polished gemstones showing a thin streak across the surface. The effect is usually caused by the particular mineral's fibrous internal structure. Also referred to as chatoyancy.

Chatoyant: An unusual effect in some polished gemstones where a thin streak of light moves across its face. Often referred to as a cat's eye.

Cleavage: The way a particular mineral breaks apart, as determined by its atomic structure. The smoothness of the resulting surface is a characteristic often used to help identify minerals. Some minerals always break along very distinct and perfect planes, while others leave ragged faces or no distinct surfaces at all.

Cold Dop: Dopping a temperature-sensitive stone with cement rather than heated wax.

Conductive Minerals: Minerals which transmit electrical currents.

Core Drill: A drill, usually diamond or carborundum impregnated, that is used to cut holes in gemstones.

Conchoidal: A fracture surface that resembles the curved and concentrically ridged inside of a shell. Obsidian and chalcedony both show nice conchoidal fractures.

Contact Zone: The region where molten rock has come in contact with cool rock.

Contact Metamorphic Zone: A region of older rock that has been metamorphically changed by contact with molten igneous material.

Country Rock: The original rock that was intruded by or overlaid by molten material.

Crown: The portion of a faceted stone lying above the girdle.

Cryptocrystalline: A mineral composed of a microscopically small crystal structures. Chalcedony is cryptocrystalline.

Crystal: A mineral's external form determined by its unique orderly arrangement of atoms. Crystals are solids, bounded by planes which intersect at specific angles.

Crystalline: A mineral that displays a distinct crystal structure.

Cubic (Isometric): A most basic of crystal structures which has three, equal-length, perpendicular axes. Minerals exhibiting cubic crystallization include, galena, halite, and fluorite. (See Chapter 4, page 38)

Cutting Materials: Those solid, fine-grained stones capable of withstanding the stresses associated with being cut and polished. Such minerals include chalcedony, agate, jade, jasper, onyx, marble, rhyolite, and serpentine.

Dendritic: A branching or tree-like pattern on a stone.

Diamond Drill: A diamond-pointed drill used to make holes in gemstones.

Diamond Paste: Diamond particles mixed into a paste compound which is smeared onto specially designed grinding and polishing wheels for use as an abrasive.

Diamond Saw: A saw used to cut stone featuring a blade whose edge has been impregnated with diamonds.

Diamond Wheel: A grinding wheel whose surface is impregnated with diamonds for better cutting than standard carborundum wheels.

Dike: An igneous intrusion that has invaded an older rock.

Dodecahedron: A crystal with twelve faces. (See Chapter 4, page 38)

Dop Stick: A metal, plastic, or wooden dowel upon which gemstones are attached while being cut and polished.

Dopping Wax: A specially formulated wax used for attaching stones to a dop stick.

Dressing: The grinding off of metal buildup covering the diamonds on saw blades and drills.

Drum Sander: A sanding wheel designed to hold sandpaper belts.

Drusy (or Druse): A rock-coating consisting of very small crystals.

Dull Luster: A surface luster of very little reflectiveness.

Dump: Where the non-valuable rock and debris is discarded at a mine site.

Earthy: A surface luster with no reflectiveness and a powdery appearance.

Eddy Current: A circular flow of water which is usually not in the same direction and sometimes even opposite the main current.

Effervescence: Gas bubbles given off when certain minerals are placed in an acid.

Etched: Pitted or scarred crystal faces which are usually the result of weathering, abrasion or natural acids.

Evaporate: Mineral or rock that was formed when a body of water evaporated.

Extrusive: Molten rock that flowed onto the earth's surface where it cooled.

Facet: One of a series of flat faces placed on a gemstone in an effort to maximize internal light reflections.

Fault: A fracture in the terrain along which opposing sides have moved.

Fibrous: A crystal type composed of tightly packed, thread-like internal crystals, such as found in asbestos.

Findings: Any of the many auxiliary parts such as bell caps, jump rings, o-rings, and pin backs used in the production of jewelry.

Fine Silver: Pure silver.

Fire: The phenomenon displayed by some gemstones which breaks up light into colors, as exhibited by precious opal.

Fissure: A separation along a fracture or break in rock.

Flatlands: The flat landscape situated below a range of mountains or hills, most frequently occurring in desert regions.

Flaw: Something in a gemstone that makes it less than perfect, such as an inclusion, chip, or fracture.

Float: Surface rock located somewhere other than where it was formed.

Fluorescence: A phenomenon exhibited by some minerals where they emit a color different from what they do under white light, when illuminated by a light of another wave length, such as ultraviolet.

Flux: A material that is applied to surfaces of metals being soldered to remove and prevent oxidation, thereby permitting a firm solder joint.

Foliated: A layering or banding displayed by some rocks.

Fortification: A type of agate that has angular, parallel lines circumscribing an inner region, similar to the walls of a fort.

Fossil: Any remnant or record of past life, such as bones, footprints, shells, or casts, that has been preserved in rock.

Fracture: A property of minerals used in their identification. Fracture is used to describe the surface appearance of a freshly broken mineral. Some terms used to describe a fracture are conchoidal, hackly, uneven, and splintery.

Freeform: Any stone which is polished into a random, non-symmetric or non-geometric shape.

Gad: A pointed, chisel-like tool which is struck by a hammer to loosen or break rock.

Geode: A generally orbicular, hollow shell often lined with crystals.

Glassy: A mineral luster exhibited by specimens with a vitreous or glass-like appearance.

Globular: A term used to describe minerals that have formed rounded, grape-like masses.

Gneiss: A banded, crystalline metamorphic rock.

Granite: A massive, light-colored igneous rock which is largely composed of mica, quartz and feldspar.

Granular: A term used to describe minerals whose surfaces appear to be made up of tiny grains.

Greasy Luster: A term to describe the luster of a mineral possessing a surface that looks like it has been rubbed with oil.

Grinding Wheel: A silicon carbide or diamond wheel used to shape gemstones.

Grits: Abrasives of various degrees of coarseness used for lapidary work. Most grit is made from silicon carbide.

Hackly: A term used to describe freshly exposed mineral surfaces that have rough or jagged surfaces, such as exhibited by cast iron and other similar metals.

Hardness: A measure of a mineral's resistance to being scratched.

Hard Solder: Gold or silver solder which requires a relatively high temperature to be melted (in contrast to soft and medium solder).

Hexagonal: A crystal system having three axes of equal length that intersect at 60 degree angles, and a fourth which is perpendicular to the others and either shorter or longer in length. Hexagonal crystallization is commonly displayed by apatite, calcite, quartz, and beryl. (See Chapter 4, page 38)

High Grade: To choose only the best stones from a large assortment of qualities.

Host Rock: A mass of rock containing other lesser types of rock or mineral deposits.

Hydrothermal: Any geological process that involves hot water solutions.

Hydrothermal Veins: A preexisting fracture within which minerals have been deposited and/or leeched out by hydrothermal action. Minerals commonly associated with hydrothermal veins include gold, pyrite, and galena.

Igneous: Rock that was formed by the cooling and resultant solidification of molten material.

Inclusion: A mineral or other substance enclosed within another mineral.

Intrusion: An igneous mass that has been squeezed into older rock and solidified.

Investment: A substance that is poured around a model to be cast in order to create a hollow replica when the model is vaporized (as in the lost wax process).

Iridescence: A phenomenon possessed by some gemstones which exhibits a rainbow play of colors.

Irregular Fracture: A jagged, nonlinear fracture in rock.

Isometric: The most regular of the crystal systems, having three, equal-length, perpendicular axes. Isometric crystals are generally cubic (six equal sides), octahedral (8-sided), and dodecahedral (12-sided). Minerals exhibiting isometric crystallization include galena, halite, fluorite, and diamond (octahedral). (See Chapter 4, page 38)

Jump Rings: Little metal rings used by jewelers to link parts together. They are made with a slit which can be closed and soldered shut after the parts have been put together.

Labradorescence: A phenomenon exhibited by some gemstones that produces reflected internal flashes, but not multicolored, as in iridescence.

Lap: A horizontally revolving plate, usually made of metal, used for grinding, faceting and polishing gemstones.

Lapidary: Refers to the craft of working with gemstones and/or a person who works with gemstones.

Lava: A molten (or once molten) igneous rock that has flowed onto the surface, often associated with a volcano.

Lenticular: Lens-shaped.

Lode: A deposit of an economically important mineral contained within solid rock.

Lost Wax: A technique for casting metals in which a wax mold is encased within a plaster-like material called an investment, heated until it vaporizes, leaving a cavity within the investment exactly like the wax mold. Molten metal is then poured into that cavity by means of little passages and, when the metal hardens, the cast can be broken, leaving a perfect metal replica of the original wax model.

Lubricant (Coolant): Any type of liquid that is used to keep lapidary machinery and/or gemstones cool when being cut, shaped, and/or polished.

Luminescence: Light given off by a mineral or rock caused by any non-heat stimulation.

Luster: The way light is reflected off the surface of a mineral. Some terms used to describe luster are metallic, pearly, dull, vitreous (glassy), silky, and greasy.

Magma: Liquified, molten rock.

Malleable: A property of some metals which allows them to be pounded and/or shaped without breaking.

Mammillary: A mineral occurrence made up of smooth, rounded masses.

Mandrel: A tapered rod used by jewelers to shape and size rings and bracelets.

Massive: A mineral occurrence in which there is no definite internal structure or form.

Matrix: The native rock within which a mineral is imbedded or attached.

Metallic Luster: A mineral exhibiting a luster similar to that of clean metal.

Metamorphic: A rock which has been substantially changed from its original state by the natural processes of extreme heat and pressure.

Microcrystalline: An internal crystalline structure so small that it can only be seen with the aid of a microscope.

Mine: An excavation done for the purpose of removing minerals from the earth.

Mineral: A natural, solid substance which has a specific chemical and orderly atomic composition.

Mineralogy: The study of minerals.

Mohs Scale: A scaled means of measuring the hardness of minerals. A Mohs hardness of 1 is the softest, while 10 is the hardest.

Monoclinic: A crystal system where all three axes are unequal in length, with two of them meeting at right angles and the third intersecting at a non-right angle, as demonstrated by gypsum and sphene. (See Chapter 4, page 38)

Mounting: The portion of a piece of jewelry that holds the gemstone.

Native Rock: The rock most prevalent to the terrain in question. The rock surrounding or being penetrated by mineral veins and deposits.

Nodule: A generally spherical mineral mass or rock sometimes filled with agate or chalcedony.

Nugget: A naturally formed, somewhat small, irregularly rounded mineral specimen, as often exhibited by turquoise and gold.

Octahedron: A geometric solid which is enclosed by eight triangular faces.

Opalescent: A mineral occurrence which displays a milky iridescence like an opal.

Opaque: Will not allow light to pass through.

Orbicular: Displays numerous circular patterns.

Ore: A mineral deposit from which a valuable metal can be profitably mined.

Orientation: The best way to cut and polish a gemstone in order to display its qualities.

Orthorhombic: A crystal system where all axes are of a different length, but they all meet at right angles. Often exhibited by topaz and barite. (See Chapter 4, page 38)

Outcrop: An exposed portion of rock. Usually refers to an exposed part of a mineral-bearing vein or deposit.

Overburden: The rock, soil and vegetation that covers a mineral deposit.

Oxide: This refers to a material's combination with oxygen, forming a new mineral, referred to as an oxide. The bright green and blue oxides of copper and the red and brown oxides of iron are good examples.

Paleontology: The science dealing with the study of fossils.

Pearly: A description of luster for minerals with surface appearance similar to a pearl.

Pegmatite: A coarse-grained igneous rock which frequently contains cavities containing large and well-formed crystals, primarily quartz, muscovite, and feldspar.

Petrifaction: A process where the original cell structure of ancient plant and/or animal is converted to stone.

Pickle: An acid bath used by jewelers to remove surface oxidation from metals.

Pinacoid: A crystal with two parallel faces. (See Chapter 4, page 38)

Placer: A glacial, alluvial or marine deposit containing concentrations of tough and heavy minerals.

Playa: A depression in a basin that is usually dry, but may sometimes contain water, such as a dry lake bed.

Pocket: A cavity or void within rock, often containing crystals.

Polishing Agents: The ultra-fine abrasive powders which are used to polish stones, such as tin oxide, cerium oxide, and chrome oxide.

Porphyry: An igneous rock which contains relatively large crystals embedded within a much finer grained mass.

Precipitate: A mineral that has crystallized or "grown" as the result of a solution evaporating.

Preform: A stone that has been trimmed to the approximate desired shape before grinding and polishing.

Primary Deposit: A mineral occurrence which is situated in exactly the same place where it was formed.

Prism: A crystal having 3, 4, 6, 8, or 12 faces, all with parallel edges, bounded by regular polygons of the same number of sides at each end. (See Chapter 4, page 38)

Prismatic: Referring to a crystal structure of a prism.

Prong: A metal tab designed to hold gemstones in settings.

Prong Pusher: A specialized jeweler's tool used to bend and secure prongs around stones being fastened in jewelry.

Propane Torch: A hand held, fine tip, propane-burning torch which is often used by silversmiths.

Prospect: A newly discovered mineral property or a partially constructed mining operation.

Pseudomorph: A mineral that has replaced and thereby taken on the geometric form of another mineral.

Pyramidal: A crystal having 3, 4, 6, 8, or 12 faces, all with non-parallel edges that meet in a single point, and bounded by a regular polygon of the same number of sides at the other end. (See Chapter 4, page 38)

Quarry: An open mining operation, generally dug into the side of a hill or mountain.

Radiating: A crystal occurrence where the crystal blades fan out from a common center. Radiating crystals are common in marcasite and wavellite.

Ravine: A small, narrow, steep-sided canyon formed by water erosion.

Rawhide Mallet: A non-scratching mallet with a specially treated leather head for use in jewelry making.

Reflection: The degree in which light waves bounce off a given surface.

Refraction: The bending of light waves as they pass from one medium to another.

Refractive Index: A numerical representation of the light refraction exhibited by a given mineral. The higher the refractive index, the more the light is bent.

Residual Deposit: Highly resistant minerals remaining after all else in the deposit has been weathered away.

Resinous: A term for luster describing a mineral surface looking like plastic or resin.

Rhombohedron: A geometric solid of six identical parallelogram faces, and opposite sides are parallel. (See Chapter 4, page 38)

Rhyolite: A fine-grained, igneous rock which is largely made up of feldspar and quartz.

Rock: Natural solids which are composed of many different types of mineral grains all fused or otherwise cemented together.

Rough: Gem material that has not yet been cut or polished.

Rutilated: A transparent or semitransparent mineral that contains needles of rutile.

Rutile: A mineral that consists of titanium oxide, usually with a little iron. It is typically reddish brown but sometimes deep red or black.

Sagenitic: Any transparent or semitransparent mineral (most commonly agate) that contains needle-like crystals of another mineral.

Sandstone: A sedimentary rock composed of tightly compacted grains of sand.

Schist: A metamorphic rock which can usually be split into thin flakes or slabs.

Scriber: A sharp tool used by lapidary artists to scratch designs onto metal.

Seam: A generally thin layer or vein containing concentrations of minerals.

Secondary Deposit: These are deposits where the minerals are found already removed from their original place of formation. That removal is usually accomplished by forces of nature, generally wind and water, and occasionally by natural chemical means.

Sedimentary: A rock formed by the compacting and cementing of sediments and debris from other rocks and animals.

Semiprecious: Gemstones that are valuable and desirable for use in jewelry, but not classified as precious.

Shaft: A vertical or inclined excavation through which a mine can be entered.

Shale: A type of fine, layered sedimentary rock formed from the deposition of silt, clay and/or mud.

Shear Zone: A small fault zone.

Silicification: The process in which organic substances such as wood and bone are replaced, cell by cell, with chalcedony or opal.

Silicon Carbide: Carborundum. A hard, synthetically manufactured substance used for grinding and sanding.

Silky: A term describing the luster of minerals displaying an appearance similar to silk. The effect is normally caused by tiny internal fibrous crystallization.

Slab: A relatively thin slice of rock which is flat on both sides.

Slab Saw: A diamond-bladed circular saw designed to cut straight slices through rock.

Slate: A metamorphic rock which has been formed by the compression of shale.

Slaty Cleavage: A property exhibited by some metamorphic rocks where they can be split into thin sheets.

Solder: An alloy, primarily of gold or silver, which will permanently join two pieces of metal when melted between them.

Soldering Blocks: A fireproof material such as charcoal, brick or ceramic upon which soldering is done.

Specific Gravity: A means of comparing the weight of a mineral with the weight of an equal volume of water. For example, if a mineral has a specific gravity of 3.5 it is three and one-half times as heavy as water.

Stalactite: A deposit resembling an icicle which hangs from a cave ceiling.

Stalactitic: A mineral occurrence which resembles an icicle.

Stalagmite: A deposit resembling an icicle built up from the floor of a cave.

Sterling: A standard alloy of silver which is composed of 92.5 parts silver to 7.5 parts copper.

Stratification: The deposition of sedimentary rock in distinct layers.

Stratum: A particular layer in a sedimentary deposit.

Streak: Streak refers to the color left on a white piece of unglazed porcelain after a mineral is rubbed on it.

Streak Plate: A white, unglazed piece of porcelain used to test the streak color of a mineral.

Striation: A mineral face with small, parallel, line-like ridges or depressions. It is commonly observed in pyrite and tourmaline.

Stringers: These are very thin mineralized veins running through another mineral or rock.

Synthetic: Artificially made mineral, but physically and chemically identical to that found in nature.

Tabular: A thin crystal which is shaped something like a tablet.

Tailings: Generally valueless waste rock from a mining operation.

Talus: Rock and gravel deposited by the forces of nature at the base of a cliff or slope.

Tarnish: The change in surface color of a mineral, usually due to exposure to air.

Template: A metal or plastic sheet containing cutouts of various shapes which are used for marking an outline onto a slab as a guide for cutting and grinding.

Termination: The end of a crystal where the face or faces come together.

Tetragonal: A crystal system where only two of the three axes are equal in length and all three axes intersect at right angles. Tetragonal crystals often produce square cross-sections. (See Chapter 4, page 38)

Tin Lap: A soft horizontally revolving metal plate (lap) upon which gems are faceted.

Topographic Map: A detailed map that shows elevations and depressions by using lines connecting points of equal elevations.

Translucent: Light can pass through but distinct images cannot.

Transparent: A mineral is transparent if it is clear and images can be seen through it.

Triclinic: A crystal system in which all three axes have different lengths and do not intersect at right angles. Triclinic crystals do not appear symmetric. (See Chapter 4, page 38)

Tumbling: A process of polishing gemstones in a revolving or vibrating barrel.

Tumbler Charges: Anything that is added to a tumbler for the purpose of grinding, polishing or cushioning. They can include grits, polish, plastic pellets, sawdust, and even soap.

Twin: An intergrowth of two or more crystals, oppositely oriented.

Ultraviolet: Light that produces shorter wave lengths than visible light.

Uneven Fracture: A fracture that is ragged or irregular.

Vacuum Casting: A rapid method of casting metals in which a vacuum-like machine sucks gases from the mold so the molten metal will flow faster and more evenly.

Vein: A thin mineral deposit which cuts through existing rock.

Vitreous Luster: A luster similar to that of glass.

Vug: A small rock cavity which often contains crystals.

Wash: A normally dry stream bed composed of sand and gravel.

Waxy Luster: A luster similar to wax, as observed in chalcedony.

Weathering: The altering of an exposed mineral or rock by the forces of wind, water, and temperature.

Wheel Cement: A rubberized cement used to attach sanding discs and polishing pads to lapidary wheels.

Zoned Crystal: An effect found within some crystals where there is a definite change of color.

APPENDIX E SUGGESTED READING

MAGAZINES

The American Mineralogist
Mineralogical Society of America
1015 18th Street N.W.
Suite 601
Washington, D.C. 20006

Gems and Gemology
Gemological Institute of America
5345 Armada Dr.
Carlsbad, CA 92008

Lapidary Journal
60 Chesnut Ave., Suite 201
Devon, PA 19333-1312

Mineralogical Record
P.O. Box 35565
Tucson, AZ 85740

Rock & Gem
4880 Market St.
Ventura, CA 93003

Rocks and Minerals
Heldref Publications
1319 18th St., NW
Washington, D.C. 20036-1802

BOOKS

Geology & Mineralogy

Arem, Joel. *Rocks and Minerals.* Geoscience Press, Tucson, AZ, 1974.

Bancroft, Peter. *Gem and Crystal Treasures.* The Mineralogical Record, Tucson, AZ, 1984.

Bates, Robert L. *Glossary of Geology.* American Geological Institute, Falls Church, VA, 1987.

Chesterman, Charles W. *Audubon Field Guide to North American Rocks and Minerals.* Alfred A. Knopf, Inc., New York, 1979.

Dietrich, R. V. *Stones: Their Collection, Identification and Uses,* 2d ed. Geoscience Press, Prescott, AZ, 1995.

Fejer, Eva and Cecelia Fitzsimons. *An Instant Guide to Rocks and Minerals.* Crescent Books, New York, 1988.

Fleischer, Michael. *Glossary of Mineral Species.* The Mineralogical Record Inc., Tucson, AZ, 1995.

Hall, Cally. *Eyewitness Handbooks: Gemstones.* Dorling Kindersley, Ltd., London, 1994.

Horenstein, Sidney, editor. *Simon & Schuster's Guide to Fossils.* Simon & Schuster Inc., New York, 1986.

Lyman, Kenny, editor. *Simon & Schuster's Guide to Gems and Precious Stones.* Simon & Schuster Inc., New York, 1986.

Maley, Terry S. *Field Geology Illustrated.* Mineral Land Publications, Boise, ID, 1994.

Pellant, Chris. *DK Handbooks: Rocks and Minerals.* Dorling Kindersley, Ltd., London, 1992.

Pough, Frederick H. *Petersen Field Guides® Rocks and Minerals.* Houghton Mifflin Co., New York, 1988.

Pough, Frederick H. *Petersen First Guide® Rocks and Minerals.* Houghton Mifflin Co., New York, 1988.

Prinz, Martin, George Harlow, and Joseph Peters, editors. *Simon & Schuster's Guide to Rocks and Minerals.* Simon & Schuster Inc., New York, 1977.

Roberts, Willard L. *Encyclopedia of Minerals,* 2d ed., Van Nostrand Reinhold Co., New York, 1990.

Thompson, Ida. *Audubon Guide to North American Fossils.* Alfred A. Knopf, Inc., New York, 1982.

Zim, Herbert S. and Paul R. Shaffer. *Rocks and Minerals.* Western Publishing Co., Inc., Racine, WI, 1957.

Field Collecting

Beckwith, John A. *Gem Minerals of Idaho.* Caxton Printers, Ltd., Caldwell, ID, 1987.

Black, Jack. *Gold Prospector's Handbook.* Gem Guides Book Co., Baldwin Park, CA, 1978.

Blair, Gerry. *Rockhounding Arizona.* Falcon Press, Helena, MT, 1992.

Butler, Gail A. *The Rockhounding California.* Falcon Press, Helena, MT, 1995.

Crow, Melinda. *The Rockhounding Texas.* Falcon Press, Helena, MT, 1994.

Crow, Melinda. *The Rockhound's Guide to New Mexico.* Falcon Press, Helena, MT, 1995.

de Lorenzo, Lois. *Gold Fever: The Art of Panning and Sluicing.* Gem Guides Book Co., Baldwin Park, CA, 1978.

Ettinger, L. J. *Rockhound and Prospectors Bible,* 3d ed. L. J. Ettinger, Reno, NV, 1992.

Feldman, Robert. *The Rockhound's Guide to Montana.* Falcon Press, Helena, MT, 1985.

Girard, Roselle M. *Texas Rocks and Minerals: An Amateur's Guide,* rev. ed. Bureau of Economic Geology, University of Texas, Austin, TX, 1964.

Kimbler, Frank S., and Robert J. Narsavage, Jr. *New Mexico Rocks and Minerals.* Sunstone Press, Santa Fe, NM, 1981.

Krause, Barry. *Mineral Collector's Handbook.* Sterling Publishing Co., Inc., New York, 1996.

Mitchell, James R. *Gem Trails of Arizona.* Gem Guides Book Co., Baldwin Park, CA, 2000.

Mitchell, James R. *Gem Trails of Colorado.* Gem Guides Book Co., Baldwin Park, CA, 1996.

Mitchell, James R. *Gem Trails of Nevada.* Gem Guides Book Co., Baldwin Park, CA, 2000.

Mitchell, James R. *Gem Trails of New Mexico.* Gem Guides Book Co., Baldwin Park, CA, 2000.

Mitchell, James R. *Gem Trails of Northern California.* Gem Guides Book Co., Baldwin Park, CA, 1995.

Mitchell, James R. *Gem Trails of Oregon.* Gem Guides Book Co., Baldwin Park, CA, 1998.

Mitchell, James R. *Gem Trails of Southern California.* Gem Guides Book Co., Baldwin Park, CA, 1996.

Mitchell, James R. *Gem Trails of Texas.* Gem Guides Book Co., Baldwin Park, CA, 2000.

Mitchell, James R. *Gem Trails of Utah.* Gem Guides Book Co., Baldwin Park, CA, 1996.

Ream, Lanny R. *Gems and Minerals of Washington.* Jackson Mountain Press, Renton, WA, 1990.

Ream, Lanny R. *Idaho Minerals.* L. R. Ream Publishing, Coeur d'Alene, ID, 1989.

Ryan, A. H. *The Weekend Gold Miner.* Gem Guides Book Co., Baldwin Park, CA, 1991.

Sanborn, William B. *Handbook of Crystal and Mineral Collecting.* Gem Guides Book Co., Baldwin Park, CA, 1987.

Sinkankas, John. *Gemstone and Mineral Data Book.* Van Nostrand Reinhold, New York, 1981.

Sinkankas, John. *Field Collecting Gemstones and Minerals.* Geoscience Press, Phoenix, AZ, 1988.

Stepanski, Scott, and Karenne Snow. *Gem Trails of Pennsylvania and New Jersey.* Gem Guides Book Co., Baldwin Park, CA, 2000.

Voynick, Stephen M. *Colorado Rockhounding.* Mountain Press Publishing Company, Missoula, MT, 1994.

Wilson, James R. *A Collector's Guide to Rock, Mineral & Fossil Localities of Utah.* Utah Geological Survey, Salt Lake City, UT, 1995.

Zeitner, June Culp. *Midwest Gem, Fossil and Mineral Trails: Great Lakes States.* Gem Guides Book Co., Baldwin Park, CA, 1999.

Zeitner, June Culp. *Midwest Gem, Fossil and Mineral Trails: Praire States.* Gem Guides Book Co., Baldwin Park, CA, 1998.

Cutting and Polishing

Cox, Jack R. *Cabochon Cutting.* Gem Guides Book Co., Baldwin Park, CA, 1986.

Cox, Jack R. *Advanced Cabochon Cutting.* Gem Guides Book Co., Baldwin Park, CA, 1986.

Dake, H. C. *The Art of Gem Cutting.* Gem Guides Book Co., Baldwin Park, CA, 1987.

Riggle, Arthur L. *How to Use Diamond Abrasives,* rev. ed. Gem Guides Book Co., Baldwin Park, CA, 1996.

Smith, Edward E. *How to Tumble Polish Rocks into Gems: Secrets of the Pros.* New London, IA, 1995.

Soukup, Edward J. *Facet Cutters Handbook.* Gem Guides Book Co., Baldwin Park, CA, 1986.

Wexler, J. *How To Tumble Polish Gemstones.* Gem Guides Book Co., Baldwin Park, CA, 1987.

Jewelry Making

Austin, Richard D., and Iva L. Geisinger. *How to Design Jewelry.* Gem Guides Book Co., Baldwin Park, CA, 1987.

Austin, Richard D. *Model Making for Jewelry Casting.* Gem Guides Book Co., Baldwin Park, CA, 1986.

Curtis, Leonard, and William A. Kappele. *Contemporary Wire Wrapped Jewelry.* Gem Guides Book Co., Baldwin Park, CA, 1995.

Dierks, Leslie. *Creative Clay Jewelry: Designs to Make From Polymer Clay.* Lark Books, Ashville, NC, 1994.

Evans, Chuck. *Jewelry: Contemporary Design and Technique.* Davis Publications, Inc., Worcester, MA, 1993.

Finegold, Rupert, and William Seitz. *Silversmithing.* Chilton Book Co., Radnor, PA, 1983.

French, Barbara. *Jewelry Craft Made Easy.* Gem Guides Book Co., 1986.

Geisinger, Iva L. *Jewelry Maker's Handbook.* Gem Guides Book Co., Baldwin Park, CA, 1986.

Jenkins, Fern, and Viola Thrasher. *How to Make Wire Jewelry.* Gem Guides Book Co., Baldwin Park, CA, 1979.

Kraus, Pansey D. *Introduction to Lapidary.* Chilton Book Co., Radnor, PA, 1987.

McCreight, Tim. *The Complete Metalsmith,* rev. ed. Davis Publishing Inc., Worcester, MA, 1991.

McCreight, Tim. *Practical Casting,* rev. ed. Brynmorgen Press, Cape Elizabeth, ME, 1990.

McGrath, Jinks. *Jewelry Making.* Chartwell Books, Inc., Edison, NJ, 1996.

Sopcak, James E. *Lost Wax & Investment Casting.* Gem Guides Book Co., Baldwin Park, CA, 1968.

Soukup, Edward J. *Jewelry Making for Beginners.* Gem Guides Book Co., Baldwin Park, CA, 1986.

Untracht, Oppi. *Jewelry Concepts and Technology.* Doubleday, Garden City, NY, 1982.

Von Neumann, Robert. *The Design and Creation of Jewelry.* Chilton Book Company, Radnor, PA, 1982.

Victor, Arthur Earl, and Lila Mae Victor. *Gem Tumbling and Baroque Jewelry Making.* Cy Johnson & Son, Susanville, CA, 1984.

Wicks, Sylvia. *Jewelry Making Manual.* Brynmorgen Press, Cape Elizabeth, ME, 1990.

Beads

Anderson, Mel. *The Basics of Bead Stringing.* Borjay, Santa Monica, CA, 1985.

Benson, Ann. *Beadwork Basics.* Sterling Publishing Co., Inc., New York, 1994.

Poris, Ruth F. *Advanced Beadwork.* Golden Hands Press, Tampa, FL, 1989.

Poris, Ruth F. *Step-By-Step Bead Stringing.* Golden Hands Press, Tampa, FL, 1985.

Ragan, Genie. *Beads: The Art of Stringing.* Gem Guides Book Co., Baldwin Park, CA, 1986.

Tomalin, Stefany. *Beads! Make Your Own Unique Jewellery.* David and Charles, Devon, England, 1988.

Wilson, Ruth. *Beautiful Beading: A Beginner's Guide.* Sally Milner Publishing, Rozelle, NSW, Australia, 1995.

Withers, Sara. *Bead Work: Start-A-Craft.* Chartwell Books, Inc., Edison, NJ, 1995.

□Photo Credits

Photo 5, page 10
   U.S. Geological Survey, W. H. Jackson, #350
Photo 6, page 12
   U.S. Geological Survey, D. H. Chapman, #204
Photo 7, page 12
   U.S. Geological Survey, J. B. Hadley, #12
Photo 9, page 14
   U.S. Geological Survey, T. N. Dale, #200
Photo 10, page 15
   U.S. Geological Survey, R. G. Ray, #54
Photo 11, page 16
   U.S. Geological Survey, C. D. Walcott, #39
Photo 14, page 17
   U.S. Geological Survey, E. S. Bastin, #38
Photo 26, page 65
   U.S. Geological Survey, J. B. Woodworth, #231
Photo 28, page 66
   U.S. Geological Survey, J.R. Stacy, #579
Photo 30, page 67
   U.S. Geological Survey, E. Howe, #57
Photo 43, page 75
   U.S. Geological Survey, O. M. Hackett, #6
Photo 44, page 75
   U.S. Geological Survey, W. B. Bull, #8
Photo 45, page 76
   U.S. Geological Survey, W. Cross, #453

□ INDEX

☐ FIELD NOTES